PENGUIN BOOKS

HARNESS HAPPINESS: PRACTICES TO HELP YOU BUILD THE SKILL OF WELL-BEING

Jenny A. Quiros is a life coach focused on helping people achieve well-being and fulfilment in life. She is a BPO industry veteran, and a Gallup Certified Global Strengths Coach and Course Leader (GCGSC); an Acceptance and Commitment Therapy Practitioner (ACT); and a Neuro-Linguistic Programming Certified Coach (NLP).

With a degree in Psychology and decades of hands-on experience leading teams for some of the world's most renowned organizations in Finance, IT, BPO and CX space, she has raised employees' engagement at work and has motivated them to achieve success both in and out of the workplace through her own brand of strengths-based leadership and empathic candour.

She is a well-being advocate and believes that the best antidote for our global mental health crisis today is to ensure that happy people stay happy. Through practical tools backed by scientific studies and simple everyday strategies, she will show you how to tap into talents and strengths that come most naturally to you—because it's in what we naturally do best that we can achieve exponential success! It is also her belief that lasting happiness and true fulfilment in life does not come from what we get, it comes from who we become, and what we are able to give because we become more!

ADVANCE PRAISE FOR THE BOOK

'Jenny's book is the fruit of both her personal and professional journeys. It is interesting to note that one of the fruits of the pandemic was an awareness of the need for a life-work balance. Jenny goes beyond balance and leads us to integration. Her book combines a process solidly grounded on professional skills and experiences and animated by a spiritual flow that comes from her own personal journey.

Howard Gardner in his book *Leading Minds* pointed out that leaders gain followers because of the story they tell, their life story in which others discover their own story.

This book will bless us with all this—integration that comes with rediscovering and reclaiming our stories.'

—Fr. Tito Caluag, executive director,
Caritas Philippines; diocese of Philippines

'Jenny Quiros brought heart, grit, and transformative leadership to TaskUs, where she left an indelible mark elevating employee engagement and building a culture rooted in empathy and performance.

In *Harness Happiness*, she brings that same energy to the page—blending psychological insight, cutting-edge science, and real-world tools into a deeply personal and actionable guide for building lasting well-being.

This isn't just another self-help book; it's a masterclass in emotional intelligence from someone who's lived it and led it. Jenny has always had a gift for helping people grow into the best version of themselves—now, she's scaling that gift to the world.

—Bryce Maddock,
co-founder and CEO, TaskUs

Harness Happiness

Practices to Help You Build the Skill of Well-Being

Jenny A. Quiros

PENGUIN BOOKS

An imprint of Penguin Random House

PENGUIN BOOKS

Penguin Books is an imprint of the Penguin Random House group of companies whose addresses can be found at global.penguinrandomhouse.com

Published by Penguin Random House SEA Pte Ltd
40 Penjuru Lane, #03-12, Block 2
Singapore 609216

Penguin Random House SEA

First English translation published by Penguin Random House SEA 2025

10 9 8 7 6 5 4 3 2 1

ISBN 9789815295443

Typeset in Adobe Garamond Pro by MAP Systems, Bengaluru, India

www.penguin.sg

To Bubi, my biggest believer, my confidence builder.
I love you always and all ways.
To Joaquin, don't ever let your big dreams scare you.
Keep showing up.
To Rafael, life is one big choreography.
Keep dancing, even when no one is watching.
To Sofia, you are the creator of your destiny.
Imagine it, believe it, build it, live it, love it.

Contents

Introduction

Well-being is a skill. It's a shift in perspective from viewing well-being as something that simply happens to us—as if by some random designation, determined solely by external circumstances which we have no control over—to viewing it instead as something we can proactively build through intentional daily practices that can grow with us over time. This perspective moves us away from the idea that life is completely out of our control, that it's merely dealt to us by some invisible hand, and that we have no other choice but to accept it as our fate.

When we look at well-being through the lens of skill-building, we become active participants in shaping the outcome of our lives, instead of just being passive recipients of our destiny.

* * *

My journey into building my own well-being as a skill began during the COVID-19 pandemic, an extremely challenging time for all of us. Everything we knew was flipped upside down, and we were all left to figure out how to outsmart an invisible enemy without losing our minds. Through the many struggles I faced during that period, I was able to put together—consciously and unconsciously—a set of strategies that made me thrive in the face of daunting uncertainty. The practices I'm sharing here are the ones I applied to myself, family members, friends, coworkers, and others who sought my help in navigating life during lockdown and our eventual transition into the so-called 'new normal'. Personally, these practices have carried me through some pretty tough situations in my life—a challenging family environment, a demanding and toxic workplace, my parents both being diagnosed with cancer within months of each other at the height of COVID-19, intense pain and grief from my dad's passing, and most recently, healing from a life-threatening disease.

I had just been diagnosed with stage 4 lung cancer when the offer to publish this book landed in my inbox. To say it was wild and unbelievable would be an understatement. It was a moment I couldn't quite wrap my head around. On the one hand, I was grappling with this devastating diagnosis, trying to process what it meant for my life, my future, my family, my everything. And then, on the other hand, there was this offer—a dream I'd held onto for so long suddenly within reach. The timing was ironic and quite frankly, cruel. I wasn't sure whether to laugh or cry. I just sat there for days in disbelief, wondering how it was even possible that two such vastly different life-changing events were colliding at the same time right before my eyes. I kept thinking to myself: *This kind of thing happens to other people, not me. People get book deals, people get cancer—but both? At the same time? To me? What are the odds of that, right?*

I had never faced a serious diagnosis before. I always enjoyed a clean bill of health and took pride in the choices I made to maintain that. I wasn't a smoker or a drinker, I practiced yoga regularly, and I was a dedicated mindfulness and meditation practitioner. I truly believed I had the stress under control. While others in my family and peer group were already dealing with hypertension, diabetes, cancer, and other chronic conditions, I felt a quiet sense of pride that, despite being in my early fifties, none of those issues had touched me.

So, you can imagine my disbelief when I received this diagnosis. No warnings, no lingering symptoms that would have hinted at something so serious lurking inside me—yet there it was! I was completely stunned. Whatever happened to stages 1, 2, and 3? And in my lungs, of all places? How on earth did I get that? Like I said, I didn't smoke, I had never been exposed to any known toxins—I made sure of that, and I hadn't experienced any lingering cough or respiratory issues. Even the doctors couldn't give me a decent enough explanation of how these things happen. They have the statistics, but never a logical explanation that made sense to my racing brain. All they could tell me for certain was that it was inoperable. The 'marbles', as I came to call them, were scattered throughout my lungs like tiny shrapnel, as if someone blasted a shotgun to my chest. Despite their caring nature and best effort to stay neutral and encouraging with their words, I could tell from the look in their eyes and the micro expressions in their faces that my prognosis was not very good.

It felt surreal. There I was, struggling to breathe, tethered to a portable oxygen machine and an indwelling medical tube in my side to drain pleural fluids from my lungs 24/7 just trying to come to terms with my new reality. How was I supposed to focus on writing a book when I could barely manage the basics of daily life? The simplest things like getting out of bed, walking across a room and taking a shower now required a bedside nurse and more energy and effort than I could have ever imagined. I had to be wheeled around the house to go from room to room. And yet, here was this dream opportunity presenting itself to me. I felt caught between two extreme realities—the sad state of my health, and on the other, this shimmering possibility of becoming a published author.

What made it harder was the glaring uncertainty staring down at me. Honestly, at that point, I didn't know if I'd live long enough to finish the manuscript, let alone see it published. Every day felt like a battle just to stay alive, to find some semblance of normalcy in a life that had suddenly become anything but normal. I had always prided myself on my resilience, on my ability to navigate life's challenges with grace and strength, but this was different.

This was not just a hurdle to overcome, this was an entirely new reality to live within. The stakes had never been higher, and the unknowns never more staggering.

I questioned whether the well-being skills I had developed over the years would be enough to get me through something like this. I had spent so much time working on building resilience, positioning it as a skill to my clients and colleagues, something I believed could help me and so many others through life's inevitable hardships. But this? This was uncharted territory for most people, including me. This was a fight I didn't know if I was ever going to be prepared for. I not only questioned whether my body and mind could endure the strain, but also whether the tools I had were enough to carry me through the crushing weight of a cancer diagnosis.

Yet, despite all the pain and uncertainty, I knew one thing for sure: I couldn't give up on either one. The fight for my life and the fight for my dream were intertwined now, and in a way, maybe they needed each other. Holding onto the idea of finishing the book gave me another reason to keep pushing forward, even when the odds seemed insurmountable. It reminded me that even in the darkest of times, life always offers a glimmer of light.

I had so many doubts, and every single one of them was completely justified. But somehow, I guess the universe had its own way of test-driving the very work I had spent years cultivating, putting it through the ultimate stress test, with me as its subject. Throwing me into the deep end to see if I would sink or swim with it was a challenge worthy of my curiosity at the very least. It felt like some cosmic experiment, pushing the limits of everything I believed in, everything I learned, everything I taught, and forcing me to live it in real time.

And so, in what I can only describe as a moment of 'impaired judgment', fuelled no doubt by a potent mix of painkillers and positivity, I signed the book deal. It felt almost reckless, like I was agreeing to something I wasn't sure was even legal. But deep down, I knew I had to do it. The calling was just too hard to miss.

With that decision made, I threw myself back into the work of finishing the book. I didn't wait for my cancer treatment to start, nor did I sit around questioning whether it was the right move. I just got to it. I figured writing would give me a sense of usefulness even as my body struggled to feel the least bit useful. I wasn't sure if I'd finish it, or even live to see it published, but none of that mattered in the moment. What mattered was showing up. Yet even that did not come easy. Some days were better than others. I would show up in front of my computer some days and write a few lines, and on other days I would just be lying in bed constructing ideas in my head because I was too weak or too in pain to even sit up. And yes, you guessed it, my chemo days were the most brutal.

Amidst the distress and unpredictability, I began crafting my 'Compelling Future List'—a list of things that would push me to show up every day and keep placing my bets, so to speak, in this game called life. A reason to live, essentially. Since I started it, the list has grown long and so compelling that not even the looming threat of death can stop me from crossing things off and adding more along the way. That list, along with the practices I write about in this book, and the overwhelming love and support of family and friends, is what empowered me to heal with remarkable speed and become a published author, both at the same time. Now, what are the odds of that, right?

* * *

This book is by no means a foolproof prescription to happiness, nor is it an antidote to death. What this book aims to share with you is the idea that we all have the ability to enrich our *quality of life*, not because of the good fortune we often find ourselves waiting to happen to us, but in spite of the messy, ugly, dysfunctional, poor little lot we think we were so unfortunate to have been handed at birth. The skills you will find here are thoughtful suggestions of how to rise above our perceived limitations as human beings.

In a world full of confusing priorities, we've somehow forgotten what we are truly capable of and what is truly important in this life. We've lost sight of our ability to nurture our inner selves, connect deeply with others, design our own future, and live with a sense of deep meaning and mindful presence. This book is about rediscovering ourselves, embracing our innate resilience, and cultivating a mindset of abundance, generosity, and gratitude amidst the flood of activities and disarray of modern life.

To me, it is not surprising that not many people realize that well-being is in fact a skill. And just like any skill . . .

. . . it can be taught

. . . it can be learned

. . . it can be increased over time, and

. . . it can be sustained throughout one's lifetime.

Much like health is also a skill that was taught to us in school through physical education, well-being develops in the same way, except, nobody taught us how to do this in school growing up.

Throughout my years of coaching people from different walks of life, I have developed this model of well-being and distilled it into five simple practices that one can easily integrate in day-to-day life. All you need is some serious intentionality, the willingness to do the inner work, and a wide-open heart ready to receive love in abundance when you finally learn how to *harness happiness*.

Here are the five simple practices you will find in the book:

1. **The practice of self-awareness**
   True self-awareness is not just about knowing what we're good at and having the language to describe what they are; that's just half of the equation. The other half is knowing how, just by being ourselves, we can affect the people around us. Everyone has unique talents, abilities, and blind spots. By recognizing and nurturing these attributes, we can achieve our fullest potential without being blind to the consequences of our actions.

2. **The practice of positive self-narratives**
   Self-narratives are the stories we tell ourselves; about our past, our present, and our future. The stories that we believe to be true become the stories we share with others. It determines the direction of our lives and the decisions that we make. Understanding your relationship with language will give you the agency to change your narrative from that of a helpless victim to a thriving life navigator.

3. **The practice of positive rituals**
   Rituals are important for us human beings because we thrive in certainty and predictability. Our brains need that. Rituals are the little things we do on a daily basis that produce results. It's what we do or don't do, what we say or don't say, what we eat or don't eat that causes us to be where we are now in our life. Repeated actions create patterns that form our reality and therefore our life. Grounding ourselves in the daily practice of gratitude and generosity is one good example. And it does not have to be material or monetary in nature. We can be generous with our time, our knowledge, and even our assumptions.

4. **The practice of mindfulness and meditation**
   The mind and the breath are the two most powerful tools we all have in our arsenal when it comes to dealing with stress. If your notion of mindfulness and meditation to this day still borders on mere mysticism, then you've been living under a rock! Scientific research in the fields of neuroscience, epigenetics, psychoneuroimmunology, and even quantum physics have shown evidence of the effectiveness of these methods in facilitating personal transformation. No yoga mat or incense required.

5. **The practice of drawing healthy boundaries**
   Healthy boundaries are a set of instructions that we communicate to the people we love (or don't love), that teach them how to have a healthy relationship with us. But don't mistake healthy boundaries for self-sabotage. When

> expectations are high and priorities are competing, the one thing that can give you clarity in decision-making are your non-negotiables. Knowing your values and beliefs is vital in boundary setting, ensuring that you don't jeopardize your own chances for success. Just remember, if you don't stand for something; you'll fall for anything!

As you explore what is possible for you in this book, you'll notice that the chapters vary in length. This is intentional and by design, reflecting the weight and complexity of each topic. Some chapters dive deeply into concepts that may take time to unpack, while others offer concise, practical tools you can integrate into your life right away. The varying lengths mirror the dynamic nature of well-being itself—some lessons call for deeper reflection, while others are simple yet powerful reminders that can shift your perspective in an instant. I encourage you to embrace this rhythm and take your time where it feels necessary, letting each chapter meet you where you are. Whether brief or detailed, every section has been crafted with the same intention: to guide and support you in building your skill of well-being.

As you turn the final page of this introductory chapter, I hope you feel inspired, energized, and curious about what's possible for you. This book isn't just about sharing my story—it's about inviting you to discover your own power to build a life of meaning, resilience, and abundance. I am beyond excited for you to dive into the practices and lessons ahead. They are not only deeply personal to me but have been tested and proven in some of life's most challenging moments. My hope is that these tools will empower you to take charge of your own well-being, no matter where you are on your life journey. Because here's the truth. The life you dream of is not a matter of chance or pure luck, it's a skill you can build—every small step in the right direction builds upon the other. So, let's begin this transformative journey together—right here, right now!

PART 1
Laying the Groundwork: Understanding Well-Being and Skill Building

Part 1 of this book, which covers Chapter 1 and Chapter 2, gently introduces the idea of well-being as more than just health or fleeting happiness—it's a deeper, more lasting sense of balance and fulfilment in all areas of life. It invites you to see well-being in a new way, not as something that simply happens by chance, but as something you can activate, nurture, and expand. By exploring what well-being truly means and how it connects to skill building through practice, this section offers thoughtful insights, personal stories, and practical tools to help you take the first steps toward creating a life filled with lasting resilience, deep meaning, and frequent moments of happiness.

CHAPTER 1

What Is Well-Being?

'Happiness can be found even in the darkest of times, if one only remembers to turn on the light.'

—J.K. Rowling, *Harry Potter and the Prisoner of Azkaban*

Most of us think we know what well-being means. We casually use the term in conversations, attach it to products and services, and integrate it into workplace programmes . It's often tied to discussions about health and happiness. But here's the truth: even experts can't agree on a singular definition of well-being. Entire fields of study are dedicated to understanding it, with scholars proposing various models and frameworks to capture its essence. Some people even confuse well-being with wellness or happiness, believing they're the same. While these concepts are related, they are not identical.

To clarify, well-being, wellness, and happiness are interconnected but distinct by itself. Wellness typically refers to physical health—things like diet, exercise, and sleep—and how they influence daily life. Happiness, on the other hand, is a fleeting emotional state that comes and goes. Well-being, however, encompasses a more holistic and enduring experience. It's about thriving—mentally, emotionally, physically, spiritually, and socially—offering a deeper, more sustainable sense of centeredness and grounding in life.

Rather than getting bogged down in academic definitions, let's keep things practical. I prefer to simplify complex ideas through comparisons. Think of well-being like a coffee machine: if it were a complicated, multi-button device, you'd likely get frustrated and give up just trying to figure out how to make the machine work. But if well-being were like a one-touch Nespresso machine, you'd find it easy and appealing, and you would likely enjoy the experience, so you make your own cup more often for the joy and ease of making your coffee on demand.

So, here's the simplest definition of well-being that resonates with me:

Well-being is a lasting state of good health, peace, and prosperity. It's the ability to cope with varying life stresses while maintaining a sense of balance and fulfilment. When your well-being is high, your feelings of happiness increase in frequency too.

Happiness, on the other hand, is a temporary emotion. It's a feeling that may arise from a great moment but doesn't last forever. However, when you focus on building your well-being, happiness becomes a more frequent occurrence as happiness arises from an inner environment of good well-being.

Well-Being as a Skill

Since happiness is clearly a by-product of having good well-being, it makes sense to work on developing the skill of cultivating your well-being. Just like mastering baking or coding, if you want more happiness, you need to put effort into building your well-being. This shift in perspective—from seeing well-being as something that happens to us based on external circumstances to something we can actively nurture—first came to me through the work of Dr Richard J. Davidson, a prominent neuroscientist and founder of the Center for Healthy Minds at the University of Wisconsin-Madison. His approach challenges the traditional view that well-being is solely determined by external circumstances, such as wealth, relationships, or career success. Instead, he proposes that well-being is largely under our control and can be developed through intentional practices. Davidson's key ideas around well-being as a skill include:

1. **Neuroplasticity: the brain's ability to change**
   Neuroplasticity shows that the brain can reorganize itself based on experience. This means that the way we think, feel, and behave can physically alter the structure of our brains. According to Davidson, practices like mindfulness, compassion, and gratitude can strengthen the neural circuits associated with positive emotions, resilience, and well-being. With consistent practice, we can train our brains to foster greater well-being, much like learning how to play an instrument or ride a bike.

2. **The four pillars of well-being**
   Davidson identifies four key skills that contribute to our overall well-being, all of which can be cultivated through practice:

   - **Awareness**: Being mindful and present in the moment. This includes being aware of your emotions, thoughts, and surroundings.
   - **Connection**: Building and maintaining healthy relationships, cultivating empathy, and showing compassion toward others.
   - **Insight**: Developing self-awareness and understanding the patterns of your thoughts and behaviours, particularly those that might be unhelpful or destructive.
   - **Purpose**: Living a life aligned with your values and having a sense of meaning and direction.

Each of these skills can be developed through daily habits and intentional focus, leading to greater overall well-being.

3. **The importance of practice**
   Like any other skill, well-being requires practice. It's not something that comes naturally to everyone, nor is it something you can achieve once and forget about. Instead, it involves consistent effort, reflection, and refinement over time. Just as you wouldn't expect to master a new language or instrument overnight, improving your well-being takes ongoing dedication. Practices such as mindfulness meditation, gratitude exercises, and compassionate actions are some examples of ways to build these skills.

4. **Well-being is not fixed**
   One of the most empowering aspects of this perspective is the idea that well-being is not a fixed trait. People often assume that their capacity for happiness or fulfilment is based on their genetics or life circumstances. I would argue that this isn't the case. While genetics and environment play a role, we have significant control over our own well-being. No matter where we start, we can always improve our well-being through effort and intention.

Well-Being and Mental Health

Well-being is directly linked to mental health. This suggests that by strengthening the skills associated with well-being, we can not only enhance our daily lives but also become more resilient to stress, anxiety, and depression. By regularly engaging in practices that promote well-being, we build emotional resilience and are better equipped to handle life's challenges.

Here are other reasons why this idea of actively cultivating well-being is fast gaining traction:

1. **Epigenetics: we can influence how our genes express themselves**
   Epigenetics is the study of how our behaviour and environment, both external and internal, influence the expression of our genes. Gene expression simply refers to genes that are 'turning on' (expressed) or 'turning off' (suppressed). While we inherit certain genetic predispositions, like a tendency toward certain illnesses, alcoholism, etc. we can influence how these genes express themselves through our choices with respect to our physical body, our energy body and our spiritual body.

   - The 'physical body' is our actual, visible body—our muscles, organs, and systems. How we take care of it with food, exercise, sleep, and medical care affects how healthy it becomes.
   - The 'energy body' is the flow of energy that moves through us, often called our life force, 'chi' or 'prana' in Eastern cultures. Practices like breathwork, meditation, and managing our emotions, especially negative emotions, help keep our energy body balanced.
   - The 'spiritual body' is our essence, our soul that connects to a higher power drawing deeper meaning and purpose for our existence. It involves our beliefs, values, and mission in this life. Things like mindfulness, prayer, or personal reflection help us nurture this part of ourselves.

   All three bodies work together to form an environment for our genes and the rest of our three trillion something cells to live and evolve in. When we make positive choices, we create a good environment inside our bodies for our systems to thrive in auspicious health and vitality. When we constantly make negative choices, we create a toxic environment for our cells that lead to chronic diseases and illnesses over time, and the choices we make for one can affect the others.

By adopting habits that support us holistically and choosing to have more positive emotions in our lives like joy, awe, and gratitude, we can affect how our genes manifest in our biology. Think of it like tending to a garden—you can't control the weather, but you can choose how you care for the soil, water the plants, and nurture their growth.

2. **Empowerment: we have control over our well-being**
   Perhaps the most empowering realization is that well-being is within our control. This mindset shifts the focus from external factors, like wealth or status, to internal factors such as our thoughts, behaviours, and choices. While we can't always control what happens to us, we have the power to decide how we respond to life's events. Understanding that we have the ability to shape our own well-being gives us a sense of control and empowerment. We are no longer at the mercy of our circumstances; instead, we are actively nurturing our well-being, and happiness naturally follows.

Positive Psychology: The Science of Thriving

Positive psychology offers a framework for understanding that well-being is more than just the absence of distress. It's about flourishing, thriving, not just surviving. This field emphasizes positive emotions, engagement, meaningful relationships, purpose, and accomplishment as core components of well-being.

Well-being isn't just about eliminating stress or sadness; it's about adding enriching elements to our life. Activities like practicing gratitude, building strong relationships, and finding purpose in daily tasks all contribute to a deeper sense of fulfilment.

Well-Being is a Lifelong Journey

The concept of well-being as a skill emphasizes that it's not a destination, but an ongoing journey. We don't reach a point where we've 'achieved' well-being and never need to think about it again. Instead, it's a continuous process of growth, adaptation, and learning. Just as our body requires regular care, so does our mental and emotional health.

The inspiring part of this perspective is that it puts the power in our hands. We are not stuck with our current level of well-being; we can consistently improve it. By doing so, we can create a life that's not only happier but also more fulfilling over the long term.

Chapter 1 Summary: What Well-Being Is

In this chapter, we took a closer look at what well-being really means and cleared up confusion around similar terms like wellness and happiness. It highlights how well-being is a deeper, more holistic experience that helps us thrive in life.

5 Key Takeaways

1. **Well-being covers all areas of life**
    - It includes your mental, emotional, physical, spiritual, and social health.
    - Well-being isn't just about one aspect of life—it's about thriving in all areas.

2. **Well-being is different from wellness and happiness**
    - Wellness focuses on physical health, like eating well, exercising, and getting enough sleep.

- Happiness is an emotion, a short-term feeling that comes and goes.
- Well-being is a more lasting state—it's about feeling balanced and fulfilled over the long term.

3. **Well-being is about thriving, not just getting by**
    - It's not just about avoiding problems or staying 'okay'.
    - Thriving means overcoming obstacles and life crises with a growth mindset, to truly get past those experiences instead of simply settling back to the way things were.
    - True well-being helps you feel grounded and connected and aware, even when life is at its hardest.

4. **High well-being is what makes life worth living**
    - When your well-being is high and strong, you handle stress more efficiently, and happiness shows up more often
    - Happiness is the natural by-product of having good well-being.

5. **A simple way to define well-being**
    - Well-being is feeling healthy, peaceful, and fulfilled despite life's imperfections.
    - It's your ability to handle life's ups and downs. It's staying balanced and focused without getting defeated.

My Final Thoughts

When you understand what well-being really means, you can start to move beyond the surface pursuit of satisfaction and instead begin to create a more fulfilling and centred life for yourself that is more reliable and enduring.

CHAPTER 2

Practice Makes Progress

> *'When perfectionism is driving, shame is riding shotgun and fear is the annoying backseat driver.'*
>
> —Brené Brown

Developing well-being is much like mastering any other skill—it requires time, effort, and persistence. Skills like emotional regulation, stress management, and resilience are teachable and learnable. When practiced regularly, these skills allow you to navigate life's challenges with greater ease.

It's important to recognize that these skills don't always come naturally. It's easy to fall into negative thinking patterns or feel overwhelmed by stress. However, with consistent practice, you can train yourself to respond more constructively, just like learning to ride a bike. Once you learn it, it becomes second nature.

Caution on Perfection

Throughout this book, you will notice that the chapters point toward the importance of various practices. Practice, in its essence, is the act of doing something repeatedly to enhance one's skill or proficiency. It's about forming habits that grow and evolve with you over time, not about achieving some mythical state of perfection. The pursuit of perfection is a seductive yet ultimately unattainable goal. This is because perfection is inherently subjective. Ask a hundred people what perfect means, and you'll get a hundred different answers. I wish someone had impressed this upon me sooner. It could have saved me years of self-reproach, both conscious and unconscious, for not being the perfect daughter, sister, wife, friend, leader, entrepreneur, whatever.

For much of our lives, many of us suffer from what I call 'closet perfectionism'. Deep down, we demand perfection from ourselves, but outwardly, we settle for being just a bit above average. This, for most of us, is a safe zone. In doing so, we unknowingly set ourselves up for our own disappointment and even self-belittlement. We think we are doing ourselves a favour by playing on the safe side of things. We're not setting our sights high enough so that when things don't turn out successful, we can say it's okay because we never really thought we would succeed anyway. It's like a self-fulfilling prophecy, all for the sake of avoiding the feeling of not being labelled as a failure.

This dichotomy creates a kind of inner conflict that contributes to a lack of clarity and direction in our lives. We hold back, afraid of being criticized, or worse, afraid of having the audacity to present something that we ourselves deem imperfect. We chase after other people's thoughts, worrying about what they might say, dreading those imagined criticisms that may or may never actually come. The irony is, we don't even know who these critics might be. Yet, we're convinced they will inevitably pull us down, and we will never recover from whatever mud they might sling our way. So, we abandon our dreams and move on to less ambitious ones, only to sabotage ourselves again and again. This becomes a repetitive cycle, one that prevents us from fully showing up in the world. At some point, we all convince ourselves that if something isn't good enough for us, it won't be good enough for anyone else either. So, we play small—not small enough to be overlooked entirely, but certainly not bold enough to run with the wolves.

I was living in this kind of pattern for a time, especially in my early adulthood. I was unaware of it at that point, all I know is that it felt safe. Eventually, 'safe' started to feel purposeless and devoid of importance and meaning. I wanted more.

The Pursuit of Excellence

It wasn't until I was introduced to the strengths practice that I realized perfection isn't the only path to being really good at something. There's also excellence. Unlike perfectionism, which seeks external validation, the pursuit of excellence is intrinsic. It's about fulfilling your own goals and motivations to the best of your ability, using your existing skills, strategies, experiences, and resources. It's not about reaching someone else's goalpost. It's about setting up your own goal posts and moving them forward as you progress, always striving for betterment and innovation.

When you own the goalpost, you feel in control, and personally accountable. This mindset allows you to become a maximizer rather than a perfectionist. It's about making the most of what's available to you at any given time, giving it your all, and then releasing it into the world—not as a perfect product, but as your best work yet. This is how personal progress is made. Do it enough times, and you'll achieve personal excellence.

On People Pleasing

'You can never please all of the people all of the time. You can only please some of the people some of the time.' My mom used to tell me this, and it has always brought me comfort whenever I find myself trying to measure up to other people's expectations. Little did I know that when my mom said 'people', she also meant me. So now, I tell myself, 'You can never please yourself all of the time. You can only please yourself some of the time.' There will always be a part of you that wants something more, bigger, better, and greater. And that's okay because you are always growing, and with growth comes the desire for improvement. Humanity has been doing this since time began; we call it evolution. It's been roughly six million years of human evolution, and we are still far from perfect as a race, but we've come a long way, haven't we?

Perfection is unattainable by design. This is how we are bred for greatness and honed into excellence. If the goalpost wasn't far enough or constantly moving, we would all be mediocre forever. The gift of imperfection is not in the striving for perfection but in the overcoming of obstacles along the way. So, keep practicing and keep striving for excellence.

Fail Forward

Fail fast and fail forward. At first glance, this might sound risky and reckless, but there's a deep wisdom in this concept. At its core, it's about vulnerability, courage, and adaptability. Failing forward is an approach that suggests when we experience failure or setbacks, we should use them as opportunities for growth and learning. Rather than seeing failure as the end of the road, we should view it as a stepping stone toward success. By analysing our failures, understanding what went wrong, and learning from them, we can adapt, improve, and ultimately move forward in a more informed and effective way.

Failure isn't something to be ashamed of or avoided at all costs. It's a natural part of the learning process. Every failure provides valuable lessons and insights that can help us progress toward our goals. By reframing failure in this way, we can cultivate a mindset that is resilient, adaptable, and focused on continuous improvement.

I experienced the wisdom of failing forward firsthand during my time in the corporate world. I had the privilege of working with some of the most talented people in the business process outsourcing (BPO) industry. One of the companies I joined was a small start-up, less than ten people working out of a cramped room above a vulcanizing shop on a provincial backroad.

Despite its humble beginnings, this company experienced a meteoric rise, eventually going public on the NASDAQ Global Select Market during the height of the COVID-19 pandemic. The company's culture was steeped in values that celebrated human potential, along with its frailties. It held a safe space for limitations to unfold naturally so that excellence could emerge through the struggle. Sensible guardrails provided clear boundaries, defining what was acceptable and what was excessive. This approach allowed our brains to say, 'Hey, it's safe here; it's time to create.'

When we don't feel safe—either psychologically or physically—our brains switch into survival mode. In survival mode, our focus shifts primarily to meeting immediate, basic needs in order to ensure our survival. This can happen in various contexts, such as during times of crisis, extreme stress, or when facing significant challenges. Here's what happens when we're operating in survival mode:

1. **Heightened stress response**
   Our bodies activate the 'fight or flight' response, releasing stress hormones like adrenaline and cortisol. This physiological reaction increases heart rate, blood pressure, and alertness, preparing us to respond quickly to perceived threats.

2. **Narrowed focus**
   Our attention becomes narrowly focused on the immediate challenges or threats at hand. Long-term goals and concerns may take a backseat to the urgent need for safety and security.

3. **Impaired decision making**
   In survival mode, our ability to think rationally and make complex decisions may be compromised. We may prioritize short-term solutions over long-term planning and overlook potential consequences.

4. **Emotional instability**
   Survival mode can lead to heightened emotions, including fear, anxiety, anger, and frustration. Coping mechanisms may vary, and individuals may experience emotional fluctuations as they navigate stressful situations.

5. **Limited resource allocation**
   Resources such as time, energy, and attention may be directed primarily toward addressing immediate threats, leaving fewer resources available for tasks that aren't perceived as essential for survival.

6. **Reduced creativity and innovation**
   Creativity and innovation often take a backseat when in survival mode, as the focus is primarily on finding practical solutions to pressing problems rather than exploring new ideas or approaches.

7. **Decreased resilience**
   While survival mode can help us cope with acute crises, prolonged exposure to stress and adversity without adequate resources for coping and support can lead to decreased resilience over time.

Failing fast and failing forward may look something like this: Do you have an idea? Throw it at the wall and see what sticks! Of course, not literally. We didn't have tubs of neon putty lying around to throw at a wall every time we had a proposition. What it meant was that we were encouraged by our leaders to ask the question, 'What if?' This question became the birthplace of innovation across many aspects of the business—from building jaw-dropping workplaces to implementing self-empowered performance assessments never before seen in the industry, and even to launching forward-thinking cafeteria programmes that prioritized not just employee health but also community well-being—including the launch of a first-of-its-kind emotional well-being programme, offering teammates access to in-house life coaching and holistic support free of charge.

To fail fast is to ride the momentum of your idea. To swim while the water is high, and the current is strong, so you'll get there faster. Internalize, socialize, and then actualize. Design it, but don't overthink it, or else analysis will paralyse you. The only way to truly foolproof a plan is to avoid being the fool who falls for it in the first place. Sharing our ideas with others and collaborating with experts was an essential part of the development process. When we finally reached a minimum viable product, we shared it with our intended users and sought their feedback. We refined it, defined what was acceptable, and then released it.

'What if?' has always been the birthplace of innovation, and it always will be the antidote to stagnation. We were creative and we were brave because we felt safe to do so. And we acted quickly on those innovations despite the fear of being judged. We took judgment as feedback, and we used it to fuel our next big idea. Over time, small wins turned into big wins. Fear seeded courage, and the results were ridiculously good.

Keep Showing Up

Have you ever had one of those days where you find yourself debating whether you should go somewhere you're expected to be? Perhaps it's a class, the office, the gym, yoga, an event, a long trip to a friend's house, or even just calling your mom. And you think, 'What's the point? Nothing is going to happen there anyway.' Well, I can tell you now that if you decide to show up, something will surely happen for you. If you don't, nothing ever will.

'Just keep showing up' is an expression I often tell my kids to encourage perseverance, consistency, and determination. It means continuing to participate, to engage, and to work towards something, even when faced with difficulties or mere inconveniences—especially when they feel demotivated or defeated by circumstances in their lives.

In various contexts, 'keep showing up' can mean:

1. **Consistency**
   Continuing to attend or participate regularly, whether it's showing up for a job, a class, a project, a social event, a family gathering, or any other commitment. Consistency often leads to progress and success over time.

2. **Persistence**
   Not giving up despite facing obstacles or failures. It's about maintaining your effort and determination even when things get tough or are simply inconvenient.

3. **Resilience**
   Bouncing back from setbacks or disappointments and continuing to pursue your objectives with resolve and determination.

4. **Commitment**
   Demonstrating dedication and loyalty to a cause, a relationship, or a goal by consistently being present and actively involved in something you believe in.

When we show up in the world, amazing things can happen. Whether it's for work, for the people we love, or for a commitment we've made, we often walk away with one, if not all, of these three things: an experience, a proposition, or a solution.

You might meet someone who offers you an intriguing proposition for a new project or collaboration that opens up new doors. Or you might find a solution to a problem you've been struggling with through a conversation with a new acquaintance at an event. The greatest of all is the experience you will gain. Experience is the ultimate teacher, and the only investment required here is your time. No time spent means nothing is learned, nothing is gained, and therefore, nothing is changed.

So, stay the course, stay engaged, and continue to put in the effort, even when it's hard or when you're tempted to opt out. This philosophy posits that success comes over time, often through persistence and perseverance. Ultimately, you'll realize that the person who benefits most from showing up isn't the people you're showing up for—it's you.

Chapter 2 Summary: The Path to Skill Building Through Practice

In this chapter, we focused on the power of practice, the drawbacks of perfectionism, and how consistency and resilience lead to personal growth. It highlights the importance of showing up, learning from failure, and embracing progress over perfection.

5 Key Takeaways

1. **Focus on practice, not perfection**
    - Growth comes from consistent effort, not chasing perfection.
    - Perfectionism often holds us back with the fear of failure, while practice helps us move forward and improve over time.

2. **Excellence is about doing your best**
    - Strive for excellence by doing the best you can with the skills and resources you already have at hand.
    - Allow your skills to grow with you over time, that's the only way they can mature.
    - Unlike perfection, which seeks approval from others, excellence is about setting and fulfilling your own goals and choosing to grow at your own pace.

3. **Failure is essential to growth**
    - Failure isn't the end—it's a valuable opportunity to learn and improve.

- 'Failing forward' means using setbacks to refine your approach and get closer to success.

4. **Keep showing up**
    - Consistency is key. Whether it's at work, in relationships, or personal goals, showing up opens doors to growth and opportunity.
    - Every time you show up, you gain experience, find solutions, or uncover new possibilities.

5. **Psychological safety fuels creativity**
    - Feeling supported and safe allows you to take risks, try new things, and innovate without fear of judgment.
    - Environments that encourage openness and vulnerability help you thrive and grow.
    - Find your tribe and surround yourself with people who want to see you succeed.

My Final Thoughts

Progress isn't about being perfect; it's about showing up, practicing, and embracing the lessons in failure. By shifting your focus from external validation to personal growth, you can cultivate resilience, strive for excellence, and create a life rich with meaningful experiences and achievements. Keep showing up—you are your own greatest investment.

PART 2
Building Your Blueprint for Harnessing Happiness

Part 2 of this book, which covers Chapters 3 to 7, guides you through five meaningful practices to help you strengthen your well-being and create a more balanced and fulfilling life. It begins with 'The Practice of Self-Awareness', inviting you to better understand yourself—your strengths, your weaknesses, your emotions, and how these play out in the world as you connect with others. 'The Practice of Positive Self-Narratives' helps you reframe the stories you have been telling yourself, empowering you to embrace possibilities instead of limitations. 'The Practice of Positive Rituals' introduces simple, intentional micro habits to bring a sense of control and stability to your days as you try to make change happen in your life. Through 'The Practice of Mindfulness and Meditation', you'll uncover the true power of your breath to calm your mind and be fully present in the now. Finally, 'The Practice of Drawing Healthy Boundaries' will support you in protecting your precious energy—making your 'yes' matter and your 'no' stick—so you can do away with resentment and focus on what is truly important to you. These gentle yet powerful practices are here to guide you on your path to healthier well-being and more frequent bouts of happiness.

CHAPTER 3

Practice Self-Awareness

> *'Knowledge is power. Knowledge about yourself is self-empowerment.'*
>
> —Dr Joe Dispenza

Authenticity and the Self-Awareness Equation

Everything starts with the self. When it comes to interacting with the world around us, the self is always ground zero. Who we are, how we perceive ourselves, and how we project that perception outward determines the quality of our relationships, the success we achieve, and the satisfaction we derive from life. Knowing yourself and who you truly are at your core is the most transformative thing you can ever do in your life.

But self-awareness isn't just about knowing your strengths and weaknesses. That's only half of the equation. The other half is about understanding how these aspects of yourself play out in the real world, how they impact others, and how they shape your interactions. It's about acknowledging both your internal landscape and the external reactions to it.

Without this second half of the equation, we risk losing sight of the broader impact of our actions, limiting our ability to grow and connect authentically with those around us. It's not enough to know you are confident, disciplined, or strategic—what matters is how these traits manifest in relationships, the workplace, and other areas of life. To put it simply, self-awareness is incomplete without an understanding of how we come across to others.

The Impact of Strengths and Weaknesses

Many people think of their strengths as the key to success. And while it's true that knowing and leveraging your strengths is crucial to thriving in both personal and professional environments, it's also important to recognize that these very strengths can have unintended consequences if not managed with awareness. In fact, it's often the overextension of our strengths that leads to some of our greatest challenges.

Let's take a positive trait like being strategic as an example. People who are naturally talented in this area can think of multiple ways to achieve a desired outcome. They're confident that their ideas can lead to success, which is undoubtedly a valuable leadership quality. However, without self-awareness, this strength can easily become a liability. A strategic leader who lacks self-awareness may overwhelm their team by presenting too many ideas at once, without offering clear guidance on priorities. The team may end up confused, with competing priorities and duplicated efforts, leading to lost time and productivity.

This isn't because being strategic is a bad trait. It's because, like any strength, it must be tempered with awareness of how it affects others. The ability to generate ideas and strategies is only as valuable as the clarity with which those ideas are communicated and executed.

Now, consider how this applies to weaknesses. Many of us believe that our weaknesses are the things that hold us back, the flaws that we need to fix or hide. But in reality, weaknesses can also provide valuable insight into our growth potential. Understanding our weaknesses allows us to find ways to work around them, seek support from others, and avoid the common pitfall of pretending they don't exist.

In fact, it's often our weaknesses that help us develop deeper empathy and understanding for others. For example, someone who struggles with time management might become more patient and understanding with others who are similarly challenged. By embracing both our strengths and weaknesses, we create a fuller, more honest picture of who we are and how we relate to the world.

The Value of Self-Awareness in Leadership

Let's return to the example of the strategic leader. A self-aware strategic leader would approach their role differently. They would understand the importance of clear communication and prioritization. Rather than dumping multiple ideas on their subordinates all at once, they would take the time to outline the most important tasks and goals, ensuring the team is aligned on the best course of action. This leader would recognize that not every idea needs to be implemented immediately—some can be held in reserve as contingency plans if the initial approach doesn't work.

Self-awareness in leadership is about recognizing not just our strengths, but also how they affect others. It's about understanding that your ideas, no matter how brilliant, won't lead to success unless they are communicated in a way that others can understand and follow. And it's about recognizing when our strengths might actually be hindering progress.

For example, a leader who is overly detail-oriented may struggle with delegating tasks, wanting to micromanage every aspect of a project. While attention to detail is a valuable trait, in excess, it can stifle creativity and growth in team members, as they may feel they are not trusted to take initiative. A self-aware leader would recognize this tendency and work to strike a balance between supervision and empowerment.

The Self-Aware Project Manager

The Background

Sarah was one of my former direct reports, a talented and driven project manager leading a high-stakes process improvement project for our operations team. The goal was ambitious: streamline workflows across multiple departments, eliminate redundancies, and improve efficiency across the board. Sarah's meticulous nature and innovative thinking made her the ideal choice for the project. However, her strong attention to detail sometimes turned into overcontrol, creating bottlenecks and hurting team morale.

The Challenge

At the start of the project, Sarah's meticulousness showed in every task. She frequently revised her team's work, held long meetings to discuss even minor details, and struggled to delegate effectively. While her intentions were to ensure success, her approach frustrated her team, who began to feel micromanaged and undervalued. Deadlines were slipping, and tension was brewing.

The Strengths Coaching Session

The turning point came during one of our Clifton Strengths coaching sessions. As we explored her natural talents and how they showed up in her work, Sarah had an 'aha' moment. We discussed how her strength in detail-oriented thinking and her problem-solving prowess was both a blessing and a curse. I helped her see how her focus on perfection, while beneficial in many ways, was inadvertently stifling her team's creativity and sense of ownership.

Sarah reflected on this and realized she had been overloading her team with too many ideas at once and was hesitant to let go of control. She recognized that her desire for high performance, left unchecked, was becoming a barrier to progress. Our coaching session helped her see the importance of balancing her strengths with awareness of how they affected others.

The Self-Awareness Pivot

Armed with this insight, Sarah committed to making three key changes in her management approach:

1. **Clarifying communication**
   She began focusing on communicating the project's top three priorities for the day in a clear and concise manner, ensuring her team understood the goals and could align their efforts.

2. **Delegating with trust**
   She consciously worked on letting go of her tendency to micromanage. She delegated tasks with clear expectations and timelines but gave her team the autonomy to approach the work in their own way. She learned to embrace the most precious rule in delegation: delegate responsibility, but never accountability. This gave her team a safe space to work creatively knowing that Sarah will always have their backs.

3. **Empowering the team**
   She allowed herself to be more generous with her assumptions of her team's capabilities as the team took ownership of their work. She encouraged them to share ideas, roadblocks they were facing and helped them get to a solution when they needed it.

Supporting Herself Through the Discomfort

Without a doubt, this self-imposed change was not a walk in the park for Sarah. She had to navigate the discomfort of changing her management style and entering uncharted territory, for her at least. She took intentional steps to support herself during this time. She leaned on mindfulness practices, starting each day with a few minutes of meditation and reminding herself to take deep breaths to calm her mind and focus her energy throughout the day. She also journaled regularly, reflecting on her progress and reminding herself why this change was necessary for both her team and her growth.

Sarah sought feedback from trusted colleagues and her team members to ensure she was on the right track, using their input as encouragement and a reality check. Most of all, she gave herself grace and kindness, recognizing that change is a process that is not always easy, and she wouldn't get it right all the time. By focusing on progress rather than perfection, she stayed motivated and resilient during this transformative period.

The Outcome

The changes were transformative. With clearer priorities, the team felt more focused and less overwhelmed. Sarah's trust in her team grew and it inspired them to take initiative and approach their tasks with renewed enthusiasm. Productivity increased as the team became more engaged and proactive. Regular check-ins allowed Sarah to stay informed and offer guidance without the need for micromanaging.

As a result, Sarah's project not only met its goal but exceeded it. Her new way of managing also left a lasting impact on her team, who felt empowered, valued, and more invested in the project's success. Beyond the tangible results, Sarah's self-awareness and growth as a manager earned her the respect and admiration of her superiors, peers, and direct reports alike.

The Lesson

Through our strengths coaching session, Sarah gained the self-awareness to recognize the impact of her behaviours and tailor her approach. It opened her up to a world of possibilities by leveraging her strengths thoughtfully. When she transformed her management style, she was able to prove that self-awareness is not just a personal asset but a vital tool for creating better outcomes and stronger teams.

Self-Awareness in Personal Relationships

Just as self-awareness plays a crucial role in leadership, it also has a profound impact on personal relationships. Take Leanne, for example. Leanne is a strong, independent woman with a host of positive attributes—she's disciplined, dependable, and resourceful. But she also prides herself on being brutally honest, to the point where she doesn't consider how her words might affect others. In her mind, being 'authentic' meant saying exactly what she's thinking, regardless of how hurtful it might be. 'I'm just keeping it real,' she says.

Leanne may think that her brutal honesty is a virtue, but in reality, it's creating a toxic environment around her. Her staff may admire her tenacity and work ethic, but they've also learned to unconsciously mirror her tactless communication style. Over time, the entire team becomes known for their harshness, which damages relationships and lowers morale. This might not seem like a problem when performance is high, but eventually, the lack of empathy and emotional intelligence will erode trust and collaboration within the organization.

What Leanne fails to understand is that authenticity isn't just about being true to yourself—it's also about being considerate of others. Authenticity without empathy is just selfishness in disguise. When we justify hurtful behaviour by claiming we're just being honest or true ourselves, we miss the point of real self-awareness. It's not enough to be honest; we must also be kind. We must understand how our words and actions affect others and adjust our approach accordingly.

In Leanne's case, her lack of self-awareness has led to isolation in her personal life. Despite her professional success, she feels unfulfilled, disconnected from her children, and unable to maintain close friendships. Her strengths of discipline, assertiveness, and independence end up working against her because she hasn't learned to temper them with empathy and compassion.

Strengths and Blind Spots

Like Leanne, we all have unique talents, abilities, and blind spots. By nurturing our positive attributes, we can achieve our fullest potential. But by recognizing the flip side of our strengths, we can take an honest inventory of our shortcomings. Self-awareness isn't about perfection; it's about being honest with ourselves, recognizing where we need to grow, and making a conscious effort to improve.

It's easy to fall into the trap of thinking that our strengths are inherently good and our weaknesses inherently bad. But the truth is, both are neutral—they only take on meaning in the context of how we use them. A strength that's overused or misapplied can become a liability, just as a weakness that's acknowledged and managed can become a source of strength.

Take empathy, for example. Empathy is generally seen as a positive trait, one that helps us connect with others and build strong relationships. But someone who is overly empathetic may struggle with setting boundaries, often putting others' needs ahead of their own to the point of burnout. Without self-awareness, this person may continue to give and give, unaware of the toll it's taking on their own well-being.

On the other hand, someone who is not naturally empathetic might be seen as cold or distant. But if that person recognizes their lack of empathy and makes an effort to develop emotional intelligence, they can learn to connect with others in a more meaningful way. The key is awareness—knowing where you stand, what you need to work on, and how to balance your strengths and weaknesses in a way that serves both you and the people around you.

Personal Story: Harnessing Empathy Without Burning Out

As someone with empathy high in my CliftonStrengths profile, I've always been deeply attuned to the emotions of those around me. Whether in my personal life or professional relationships, I could sense others' feelings with an almost visceral clarity. This ability often made me a trusted confidant and a source of comfort for those who needed someone to lean on. My intuition would often guide me in knowing exactly what to say or do to ease someone's burden. However, this gift came with its challenges—challenges I wasn't always aware of, much less prepared to navigate.

My Challenge

One particularly demanding period of my coaching career involved working with clients going through a deeply emotional family crisis. Every session felt heavy, as they unpacked layers of grief, frustration, and self-doubt. As their coach, I was fully present, holding space for their pain and helping them navigate their way forward. But my high empathy made it impossible for me to leave their emotions behind after our sessions. I carried their sadness, their fears, and their struggles with me, replaying our conversations in my mind and second-guessing if I had done enough to support them.

This wasn't unique to one client. As my schedule filled with emotionally charged sessions, I began to feel drained. I was always trying to find solutions for problems that weren't mine to solve. I stopped prioritizing my own needs because I felt guilty setting boundaries. My emotional bandwidth stretched thin, and my work—something I once enjoyed so much—started to feel like a burden. My natural instinct was to give endlessly because I couldn't stand the thought of them feeling alone or unsupported.

Initially, I felt good about being able to help. But over time, I started to notice changes in myself. I felt drained emotionally, physically, and mentally. My own needs began to take a backseat as I prioritized my clients' feelings and well-being over my own. Without me realizing it, I stopped setting boundaries because it felt selfish to say 'no' when someone else was hurting. Exhaustion crept in, and I became irritable, unfocused, and detached from my own needs and my health began to suffer.

The turning point came when my husband noticed the change in me. During a conversation, he gently pointed out that while my empathy was one of my greatest strengths, it seemed to be taking a toll on me. He used a phrase I'll never forget: 'Mrs Owl, you need to get unstuck.' His words hit me hard. I realized I had been so focused on helping others that I had completely neglected my own sanity and well-being.

This moment of self-awareness was very uncomfortable but necessary. I began to see how my empathy, while a powerful strength, had also become a source of weakness for me. I had to accept that my inability to set boundaries wasn't noble—it was unsustainable. My constant giving wasn't just hurting me; it was diminishing the quality of support I could offer.

My Path to Balance

I started taking intentional steps to regain balance and protect myself from burnout. Here's what helped:

1. **Setting emotional boundaries**
   I learned that saying 'no' doesn't make me less empathetic. I practiced setting limits on my time and emotional energy, recognizing that I couldn't pour from an empty cup. I reminded myself that while I could walk alongside my clients on their journey, I couldn't carry their burdens for them. I learned to 'leave the work at work', creating a heart-centred boundary between my role as a coach and my personal life.

2. **Practicing self-care**
   I made self-care a non-negotiable for me, carving out time to recharge through activities like meditation and mindfulness, healthy food choices, and some physical exercise. These practices helped me reconnect with myself and replenish my energy.

3. **Seeking support and learning to trust**
   I allowed myself to lean on others more. Honestly, this was one of the hardest things for me to do. I have always been the go-to person, so me going to someone for support was rarely the case. But I decided to embrace it. I realized that in the case of someone who has high empathy like me, a space to unload emotions I absorbed from others was an important skill I needed to develop. More than that, learning to trust others with my most vulnerable feelings turned out to be most liberating.

4. **Distinguishing empathy from responsibility**
   I started to recognize the difference between being empathetic and taking on someone else's emotional burden. While I could support others, I wasn't responsible for fixing everything for them.

5. **Adopting a growth-oriented perspective**
   I reframed my role as a coach. My job wasn't to solve my clients' problems but to empower them to find their own solutions. This shift allowed me to support them fully without feeling entirely responsible for their outcomes.

The Lessons I Learned

This experience taught me that strengths, even those as celebrated as empathy, can become barriers when overused or unchecked.

Self-awareness helped me recognize when my empathy was working against me and allowed me to make changes that not only protected my well-being but also improved the quality of support I could offer to others.

Now, I understand that caring for myself isn't selfish—it is essential. When my empathy cup is full, I can give freely without resentment or exhaustion.

As a coach, empathy still remains one of my greatest strengths, but now I use it with intention and balance. I've learned that true compassion includes turning that compassion towards myself, and that setting boundaries doesn't diminish my empathy—it amplifies it. As a result, I've become not just a better supporter of others but also a more resilient and self-aware version of myself.

Cultivating Self-Awareness

So how do we cultivate self-awareness? It's not something that happens overnight—it's a lifelong process that requires introspection, feedback, and a willingness to learn from experiences. Here are some practical steps you can take to develop greater self-awareness:

1. **Reflect on your experiences**
   Take time each day to reflect on your interactions, your emotions, and your thoughts. What went well? What didn't? How did you feel, and how do you think others felt? By regularly reflecting on your experiences, you'll start to notice patterns in your behaviour and gain insight into how you come across to others.

2. **Seek feedback**
   Self-awareness doesn't happen in a vacuum. Ask for feedback from trusted friends, family members, or colleagues. Be open to their insights and use them to gain

a more accurate picture of yourself. Remember, the goal isn't to change who you are, but to understand how you can show up more effectively in your relationships.

3. **Practice mindfulness**
   Mindfulness is the practice of being present and fully engaged in the moment. By practicing mindfulness, you can become more attuned to your thoughts, emotions, and reactions, which is a crucial part of developing self-awareness. When you're mindful, you're better able to recognize when you're acting out of habit or reacting unconsciously, and you can choose to respond in a more intentional way.

4. **Take responsibility for your actions**
   Part of self-awareness is recognizing that you are responsible for your actions and their impact on others. If you've hurt someone, own up to it. If you've made a mistake, learn from it. The more you take responsibility for your actions, the more self-aware you will become.

5. **Stay open to growth**
   Self-awareness isn't a destination; it's a journey. As you go through life, you will continue to learn more about yourself and how you interact with the world. Stay open to growth and be willing to adapt and change as you gain new insights.

In the end, authenticity is not about being brutally honest or refusing to change. It's about understanding who you are, how you come across to others, and how you can show up in a way that is both true to yourself and respectful of those around you. True authenticity requires a deep commitment to self-awareness, and it is through this commitment that we can create a life that is not only successful but also deeply fulfilling.

The Language of Strengths

I'm a big advocate of the strengths practice, not just at work but also in my personal and family life. This belief isn't solely because I'm a Gallup Certified Global Strengths Coach and Course Leader, but because long before I encountered the Gallup CliftonStrengths assessment, I was already drawn to focusing on people's strengths rather than their weaknesses. In fact, it's no surprise that my top theme in the CliftonStrengths assessment is Maximizer. I naturally love taking things from good to great. Like a homing device, I instinctively seek to optimize and maximize resources and potential, always focusing on what people are naturally good at instead of dwelling on their shortcomings.

CliftonStrengths is a highly regarded assessment tool developed by Gallup that helps individuals identify their unique talents and strengths. The assessment identifies thirty-four dominant talent themes, which represent specific patterns of thought, feeling, and behaviour. It operates on a core principle that people excel when they invest in their strengths rather than spending time and energy trying to fix their weaknesses. According to the research, recognizing and cultivating these talents can lead to greater personal and professional fulfilment.

The focus on strengths is transformative. By embracing strengths-based development, individuals and teams can move from being merely competent to truly thriving. This practice empowers people to lean into their natural talents, fostering growth, engagement, and success. For me, this is more than just a professional philosophy, it's a personal conviction that shapes how I approach everything from leadership to coaching to parenting. In my own journey, I've seen firsthand the profound impact of recognizing and nurturing strengths, and I continue to believe that this approach is key to unlocking not only potential but also a greater sense of purpose and fulfilment.

If you are not so inclined to invest in a paid assessment, there are several ways to identify one's strengths without using copyrighted tools or formal assessments. Here are some practical ways you can 'mine' for strengths in your life to help uncover natural abilities, patterns, and talents:

1. **Reflect on peak experiences**
    - Look back on times when you felt 'in the zone', accomplished, or proud of your work. Instead of only thinking about tasks or roles, consider the qualities and attitudes you brought to those moments.
    - Questions to ask: *What skills did I rely on? What personal qualities surfaced in this experience (e.g., patience, curiosity, problem-solving)?*
    - Example: If you recall a time when you led a project that went smoothly, the strengths might include organization, adaptability, or motivational skills.

2. **Notice patterns in feedback from others**
    - Seek out both formal and informal feedback. Take note of how friends, colleagues, and even family members describe your contributions or personality.
    - Questions to ask: *What do people often thank me for? What strengths do they seem to notice that I might overlook?*
    - Example: If you're repeatedly told you have a calming presence, explore how you use listening or empathy in daily life.

3. **Explore moments of flow**
    - Flow states occur when you're so engaged that time seems to slip away. Identify activities where you're highly focused and feel an effortless sense of competence.
    - Questions to ask: *When do I feel most immersed in my work or hobbies? What about these moments feels so engaging?*

- Example: If you experience flow while teaching or explaining ideas, you might have strengths in communication or teaching.

4. **Analyse successes and achievements**
   - Reflect on your past accomplishments and pinpoint specific strengths that contributed to each success.
   - Questions to ask: *What was my role in this achievement? What challenges did I navigate well?*
   - Example: If you've received praise for a project that you completed solo, the strengths could be independence, problem-solving, or perseverance.

5. **Ask friends, family, or colleagues**
   - Reach out to those who know you well. Ask them to share not only your strengths but also unique qualities that distinguish you from others.
   - Questions to ask: *What do you think I'm naturally good at? When have you seen me at my best?*
   - Example: If a friend says you're resourceful, this might point to strengths in innovation, resilience, or strategic thinking.

6. **Reflect on what comes easily to you**
   - Strengths often feel natural and don't require a lot of effort. Reflect on skills or tasks where you feel particularly efficient.
   - Questions to ask: *What tasks do I complete faster or more easily than others? Where do I feel in my element?*
   - Example: If you find yourself quickly grasping new software, you might have strengths in technical adaptability or learning agility.

7. **Notice what drains or energizes you**
   - Observe your energy levels before, during, and after different tasks. Strength-aligned tasks typically feel fulfilling and less tiring.
   - Questions to ask: *Which activities leave me feeling energized? Which ones feel draining, even if they're easy?*
   - Example: If you feel excited after brainstorming sessions, creativity and ideation may be your core strengths.

8. **Keep a strengths journal**
   - A strengths journal allows you to document daily experiences, focusing on times when you felt particularly effective or satisfied.
   - Questions to ask: *What did I do today that felt aligned with my abilities? What moments stood out as high points?*
   - Example: Journalling about a successful meeting might reveal strengths in communication or leadership.

9. **Identify recurring themes in problem-solving**
   - Consider how you approach challenges. Do you tend to break down problems analytically, or do you prefer brainstorming solutions?
   - Questions to ask: *What steps do I naturally take when facing a problem? What role do I often play in group problem-solving?*
   - Example: If you instinctively break down complex problems, strengths might include analytical thinking or strategic planning.

10. **Consider what others rely on you for**
    - Think about the roles you often assume in various settings, such as at work, home, or in your community.

- Questions to ask: *What roles do people often ask me to take on? What strengths do they see in me that encourage this reliance?*
- Example: If you're frequently asked to organize events, you might have strengths in logistics, organization, or event planning.

11. Use the 'energy audit' technique

- Review your day-to-day activities and note which ones consistently leave you feeling energized or fatigued.
- Questions to ask: *What tasks naturally motivate me? Which tasks feel like they deplete my energy, even if they're easy?*
- Example: If collaborating with others always energizes you, strengths may lie in teamwork, communication, or relationship-building.

12. Observe your interests and curiosities

- Identify hobbies, books, or activities that you're drawn to without external motivation, as these interests often align with strengths.
- Questions to ask: *What topics do I explore without being prompted? What activities would I pursue even if they weren't required?*
- Example: If you're consistently curious about new technology, this could indicate strengths in innovation or technical adaptability.

13. Reflect on past struggles and lessons learned

- Examine challenging situations and consider what strengths emerged as you overcame obstacles or adapted.
- Questions to ask: *What positive qualities did I rely on in difficult times? What lessons have I learned that point to core strengths?*
- Example: If you managed a stressful situation through empathy, your strengths might include emotional intelligence or compassion.

Chapter 3 Summary: The Practice of Self-Awareness

In this chapter, we explored the transformative power of self-awareness and its profound role in shaping our relationships, leadership styles, and personal growth. It highlights that true self-awareness isn't just about knowing who you are, it's also about understanding how you show up in the world and the impact your words and actions have on others. By finding a balance between internal insight and external awareness, we unlock the ability to live more authentically and lead more effectively, without being misunderstood.

5 Key Takeaways

1. **Self-awareness is the foundation of authenticity**
    - Knowing your strengths, weaknesses, and core values is only half of the equation.
    - True self-awareness combines internal understanding of who you are with an appreciation of how your behaviours and decisions land in the world and affect others around you.

2. **Strengths without awareness can become weaknesses**
    - Strengths are essential for success, but when misused, they can create unintended consequences.
    - Confidence, when unchecked, can come across as insensitivity and arrogance, alienating others and creating barriers to trust and collaboration.

3. **Weaknesses offer growth potential**
    - Weaknesses are not limitations, they are opportunities to grow, adapt, and connect more deeply with others.
    - By acknowledging your areas of weakness, you can create strategies to address them and even leverage them as tools for greater empathy and understanding.

4. **Self-aware leaders build stronger teams**
    - Leadership isn't about having all the answers; it's about understanding how to balance your strengths with clear communication and trust.
    - Leaders who prioritize self-awareness create environments where others feel empowered, valued, and inspired to contribute.

5. **Authenticity is a balancing act**
    - Authenticity isn't about unfiltered honesty or 'just being yourself' without considering the impact.
    - It's about aligning your actions with your values while being considerate of others, creating trust and connection in both personal and professional relationships.

My Final Thoughts

Self-awareness is not a one-time revelation but an ongoing practice of reflection, feedback, and growth. It allows us to understand who we are at our core and allows us to see clearly the impact we are making on the world around us. When authenticity is paired with self-awareness it creates a powerful synergy that strengthens relationships, enhances leadership, and fosters a deeply meaningful, fulfilling life for you.

CHAPTER 4

Practice Positive Self-Narratives

> *'The only person you are destined to become is the person you decide to be.'*
>
> —Ralph Waldo Emerson

Harnessing the Power of Your Personal Story

Self-narratives are the stories we tell ourselves; about our past, our present, and our future. The stories that we believe to be true become the stories we share with others about who we are. It determines the direction of our lives and the decisions that we make. Understanding the language that we use to form those stories gives us the agency to change not just our narrative but our lives and the value that we place on the events and circumstances that made us who we are now. Changing our narrative does not mean lying about our past, it is about reframing our past experiences in a way that is empowering rather than self-defeating. Language has the ability to transform our personal history from that of a helpless victim to one of a strong and thriving life navigator.

Yes, I consciously used the word 'thriving', instead of the word 'surviving' to demonstrate the power of positive language.

The difference between a survivor and a thriver often lies in how they approach hardships and the thought patterns they adopt toward challenges they encounter.

The Survivor

- *Mindset*: A survivor's mindset is directed at overcoming adversity and merely 'getting through' tough experiences. Their effort and energy are typically spent managing obstacles in a manner that ensures nothing more than survival and safety.
- *Focus:* Their primary focus is on endurance in order to maintain a bare minimum state of mental and physical well-being. They react, rather than respond to the problems life throws at them and tend to do only what's necessary to keep their head above water.
- *Growth:* While survivors may gain strength and resilience from their struggles, their goals are typically centred around restoration rather than expansion. They tend to settle at healing and recovery rather than pushing beyond the boundaries of their current circumstances and creating a better future for themselves.
- *Outlook:* Survivors are about persistence, grit, and resilience but often with a sense of having been 'worn down' by the process.

The Thriver

- *Mindset:* A thriving life navigator actively seeks out opportunities for self-improvement, even in the face of adversity. They approach difficulties with curiosity, adaptability, and optimism. Thrivers view challenges as potential paths to life enrichment.
- *Focus:* Thrivers focus on finding ways to flourish and evolve despite, or even because of, the challenges they are facing. They are proactive rather than reactive. They are intentional in their search for meaning, joy, and fulfilment in their lives.

- *Growth:* Thrivers don't only adapt to difficult situations, they also maximize those experiences to improve, learn, and expand their potential. The desire to become a better individual is continuous and expansive.
- *Outlook:* Their view of the future is one of abundance and limitless possibility. They not only live through tough experiences but emerge from them stronger and wiser. Thrivers hold a deep knowing that they have the ability to actively shape their lives for the better no matter the circumstances.

The key difference is that surviving is about *endurance*—which can become exhausting at some point. Thriving, on the other hand, is about *transformation*—which is an inspired way of living that is beyond surface level change. It's about internal shifts that lead to new and expanded ways of being.

Personal Story: Breaking The Scarcity Cycle

Before embarking on the transformative journey of practicing positive self-narratives myself, I used to share my life story with an underlying theme of scarcity. Whenever someone would say 'tell me about yourself', or if I found myself sharing my story with anyone willing to listen, my narrative was consistently rooted in a sense of lack. This sense of scarcity was not merely about material possessions, it permeated every aspect of my life, influencing my self-perception, my relationship choices, every important decision I made in my career, and my overall outlook on life.

My Early Life: The Roots of Scarcity

I grew up in a world where resources for our family were always limited. We were not destitute, but the feeling of 'never enough' was a constant presence. At one point, my family was financially stable, but a series of unfortunate events stripped us of that stability. My parents, despite their hard work and perseverance, lost everything almost overnight. This abrupt change marked the beginning of a life defined by scarcity for me.

Yet, within this environment of financial struggle, my family remained loving, close-knit, and supportive. We faced challenges together, and my childhood, despite the lack of material wealth, was filled with enduring happy memories. I take great pride in the resilience and determination of my parents, who were never too proud to engage in any sort of honest work to provide for our daily basic needs. Their example taught me the value of hard work and the importance of family. These lessons became a core part of my identity.

However, along with these positive lessons, I also internalized the notion that scarcity was an inherent part of life. My father grew up in scarcity, my mother did as well, and naturally, I was raised in the same environment and conditioned by my parents, consciously or unconsciously. Over time, I began to wear this scarcity as a badge of honour, allowing it to define who I was. Scarcity became my identity, shaping my beliefs, behaviours, and expectations of what life could offer.

The Manifestation of Scarcity in Adulthood

As I transitioned into adulthood, the narrative of scarcity that I had internalized during my childhood began to manifest in various aspects of my life. The universe, in its mysterious ways, seemed to reinforce this theme in my life, ensuring that it remained a constant presence. Financially, I was always struggling and perpetually broke because money and opportunities appeared to be scarce. In my relationships, I consistently found myself being cheated on, magnifying my lack of confidence in myself and my lack of trust in others. My health also suffered, as I often lacked the time and resources to prioritize proper nutrition and exercise, leading to a body that mirrored my scarcity mindset; in its lack of health and vitality as it were.

Life felt like a river of scarcity, and I was swimming against the current, exhausting myself in the process. I believed that if I could just swim hard enough and fast enough, I would eventually reach the open ocean of abundance that I so desperately sought. But the harder I struggled, the more entrenched I became in this mindset of lack. In my subconscious mind, the idea that financial deprivation was synonymous with strong family bonds and happy childhoods was deeply ingrained. My subconscious mind believed that had I not grown up in scarcity, my life might have taken a different, perhaps worse, turn—one where material abundance led to a broken family, an unhappy childhood, and perhaps a lack of drive and ambition.

This belief was reinforced in me by societal narratives that often paint wealth as the root of all evil, laziness, entitlement, and broken relationships. I convinced myself that financial struggle was somehow noble, that it built character and most importantly, kept my family close and intact. But the reality is that these issues—the broken homes, the addiction, the dysfunction, the lack of ambition—are not exclusive to the wealthy. It does in fact happen to anyone, regardless of their financial and social situation. Rich or poor, both can be afflicted by these challenges—that's just life. It took me a long time to realize that the narrative I had constructed in my mind was not a universal truth but rather a stark reflection of my own limiting beliefs.

The Subconscious Reinforcement of Negative Narratives

The human mind is a powerful thing. It is capable of shaping our reality based on the stories we tell ourselves. My subconscious mind, wrapped up in the narrative of scarcity, ensured that I remained consistent with this belief system. Here is how it showed up for me: whenever I came into money, I would find ways to spend it all or give it away, often to family members. While generosity is not inherently negative, in my case, it was a means of reinforcing my subconscious belief that I was destined to be broke or else my family will somehow be doomed to fail. By unconsciously depleting my resources, I kept myself in a state of financial struggle, unable to break free from the cycle of scarcity and therefore staying true to my subconscious programmes , aka my identity.

In relationships as a young adult, I would subconsciously sabotage my chances of happiness by becoming emotionally unavailable. My deep-seated belief that I was 'not enough' led me to pull away from partners who might have loved and valued me for who I am. As Brené Brown so aptly puts it, I kept telling myself 'I am not enough and therefore not worthy of love and belonging.' This belief was a cornerstone of my scarcity mindset, leading me to engage in behaviours that reinforced my sense of inadequacy, again aka my identity.

Even in my professional life, the scarcity mindset held me back many times. Opportunities for growth and advancement were met with self-doubt and fear of failure. I believed that professional success was something that happened to others, not to someone like me, who was destined to struggle. This self-sabotaging behaviour kept me in jobs that were unfulfilling and underpaying, further cementing the narrative that I was not worthy of abundance.

Shifting the Narrative: My Journey Towards Self-Empowerment

The turning point in my life came from a very providential source—my godmother, Meredith. She shared with me a piece of wisdom that would eventually become the catalyst for change in my life. She said, *'Broke is temporary, but poor is eternal.'* This statement struck me to the core and lingered in my heart and mind for years. She explained that my family could never get out of scarcity because we seem to have the willingness to suffer but we didn't have the willingness to sacrifice. This distinction puzzled me at first, and I struggled with it for a long time. I wasn't sure what to make of it, let alone act on it.

It wasn't until later in life that I finally came to understand that the statement 'broke is temporary, but poor is eternal' highlights the difference between a temporary lack of money (being broke) and a chronic state of financial struggle (being poor). When someone is broke, they may lack resources at the moment, but they have the potential to improve their situation through hard work, smart choices, and sometimes a bit of luck. Being broke is a temporary condition that can be overcome with time and inspired effort.

Being poor on the other hand, implies a more enduring state of financial hardship, often rooted in systemic issues such as low-paying jobs, structural inequalities, or an overdependence on external assistance. Poverty is not just about lacking money; it is about lacking the means and the sincere willingness to change one's circumstances for the long term. The real challenge here lies in the mindset that accompanies poverty—a mindset that perpetuates the cycle of financial struggle and keeps individuals trapped in a state of lack. What makes poor eternal is not just the absence of money but the presence of a 'poor mentality'. This mindset is characterized by beliefs, attitudes, and behaviours that reinforce financial struggle. Individuals with a poor mentality often see the world through the lens of scarcity, believing that resources are limited and that there will never be enough to go around. This type of mindset leads to hoarding, selfishness, fear of taking risks, and an inability to seize opportunities that could otherwise improve their lives.

Having said all that, I also later realized that one doesn't have to be living along the poverty line to feel lack. One can in fact be extremely wealthy in life and still have a scarcity mindset. And trust me when I say, this too leads to hoarding, selfishness, fear of taking risks, and an inability to seize opportunities that could otherwise expand their wealth rather than sit on it and fear for the next wave of inflation or crash in the financial system.

Breaking Free from the Poor Mentality

I realized then that understanding and addressing the poor mentality is what was needed to break free from the cycle of scarcity I was in. The poor mentality is not just about financial habits; it encompasses a broader set of beliefs and behaviours that affect every aspect of our life. Here are some common characteristics of the poor mentality and how they can be transformed into a mindset of abundance:

1. **Scarcity mindset vs. abundance mindset**
   A scarcity mindset is rooted in the belief that resources are limited, leading to fear, anxiety, and a focus on what is lacking. Individuals with a scarcity mindset may struggle to invest in their future, as they are focused on merely getting through the present.

   To shift to an abundance mindset, it is crucial to recognize that the world is full of opportunities and resources. An abundance mindset embraces the idea that there is enough for everyone, and that success is not a zero-sum game. This mindset encourages individuals to take risks, invest in their growth, and share resources and opportunities with others. By focusing on possibilities rather than limitations, an abundance mindset opens the door to more opportunities and greater fulfilment.

2. **Short-term thinking vs. long-term visioning**
   The poor mentality often involves short-term thinking, where immediate gratification takes precedence over long-term goals. This mindset can lead to impulsive decisions, such as spending money on non-essential items instead of saving or investing in the future. Short-term thinking keeps individuals trapped in a cycle of financial struggle, as they are unable to build the foundation for long-term success.

Shifting to a long-term vision requires a change in priorities. It involves setting clear goals for the future and making decisions that align with those goals. This might mean delaying immediate gratification in favour of long-term gains like getting an education, upskilling for career advancement, or saving up to attain financial stability. A long-term vision empowers individuals to make choices that lead to lasting success and fulfilment.

3. **Dependency vs. self-reliance**

A poor mentality can foster a sense of dependency on others or external assistance, such as welfare programmes, charitable organizations, loan sharks, or rich parents and relatives. While there is nothing wrong with seeking help when needed, a mindset of dependency can prevent individuals from taking proactive steps to improve their situation over time. This dependency often leads to a sense of powerlessness and a belief that one's circumstances are beyond their control. What's worse is that it can lead some people to believing that staying poor is in fact advantageous, because it forces those who have more to keep giving more, in other words, they get to take advantage of the system or anyone for that matter.

Cultivating self-reliance involves taking ownership of one's life choices and making decisions that lead to independence. This doesn't mean rejecting help altogether but rather using it as a stepping stone towards self-sufficiency. Self-reliance is about recognizing that one has the capacity to create change by taking action to improve one's circumstances. It is about building the skills, knowledge, and confidence needed to navigate life's challenges independently.

4. **Lack of financial literacy vs. financial empowerment**
A poor mentality often includes a lack of financial literacy, which can lead to poor decision-making and vulnerability to financial pitfalls. Without a solid understanding of budgeting, saving, and investing, individuals may struggle to manage their money effectively and miss out on opportunities to build wealth.

Financial empowerment begins with education. Learning the basics of personal finance—such as how to create a budget, manage debt, and invest for the future—can transform one's relationship with money. Financial empowerment also involves developing a mindset of abundance, where money is seen as a tool for creating the life one desires, rather than a source of stress and anxiety.

5. **Negative self-talk vs. positive self-narratives**
Negative self-talk is a hallmark of the poor mentality. Individuals with this mindset may have low self-esteem and feelings of hopelessness about their ability to change their circumstances. This negative self-talk reinforces the belief that they are incapable of achieving success and that their current situation is permanent.

Shifting to positive self-narratives involves rewriting the stories we tell ourselves about who we are and what we are capable of. It requires challenging negative beliefs and replacing them with affirmations of strength, resilience, and potential. Positive self-narratives empower individuals to take control of their lives and pursue their goals with confidence and determination.

6. **Avoidance of responsibility vs. ownership of choices**
A poor mentality often involves avoiding responsibility for one's circumstances. Individuals may blame external factors—such as their upbringing, societal barriers, or bad

luck—for their financial struggles. While these factors can certainly play a role, avoiding responsibility prevents individuals from taking control of their lives and making the changes necessary to improve their situation.

Taking ownership of one's choices is a powerful step towards empowerment. It involves acknowledging the role that one's decisions and actions play in shaping their reality. By taking responsibility, individuals can identify areas for improvement and take proactive steps towards achieving their goals. Ownership of choices also fosters a sense of agency and control, empowering individuals to create the life they desire.

Rewriting the Self-Narrative: My Journey of Transformation

The process of shifting from a scarcity mindset to an abundance mindset is not easy, and it does not happen overnight. It requires a deep level of self-awareness, a willingness to confront and challenge deeply ingrained beliefs, and a commitment to personal growth and transformation.

For me, the journey began with recognizing the patterns in my life that were perpetuating scarcity. Knowing that made me aware of the areas that I needed to work on and gave me the confidence to make a conscious choice to rewrite my skewed self-narratives. One of the first steps in this journey for me was changing the way I spoke to myself. Instead of reinforcing the idea that I was destined to struggle, I began to affirm my ability to create abundance in my life. I started to believe that I was worthy of love, belonging, success, and financial stability. This shift in mindset allowed me to approach life with a sense of possibility rather than limitation.

In my relationships, I worked on building self-esteem and developing a sense of self-worth. I learned to value myself and set boundaries that protected my emotional well-being. This allowed me to form healthier, more fulfilling relationships, where

I no longer felt the need to pull away or sabotage my chances of happiness. I had to teach myself how to gracefully be open to receiving and being grateful for everything that comes my way.

Perhaps most importantly, I embraced the idea that life is not a struggle against scarcity but a journey towards abundance. I stopped seeing life as a river I had to swim against and started to flow with it, trusting that the universe would provide what I needed as long as I remained open to receiving it. This shift in perspective allowed me to approach challenges with a sense of calm and confidence, knowing that I had the power to create the life I desired.

My Ongoing Journey of Empowerment

My journey from a scarcity mindset to an abundance mindset is an ongoing one, and it requires constant self-reflection and growth. While I have made significant progress in rewriting my negative self-narratives, there are still, and will always be, moments when old patterns and beliefs will resurface. However, I have learned that change is inherently uncomfortable, and it feels unfamiliar. Our knee-jerk reaction to this is to go back to the familiar because then it feels safe. It's in those moments when I know I am changing. So, I take in these moments and label them as opportunities for growth, instead of calling them setbacks. Each time I confront and overcome a limiting belief I move closer to living a life of true abundance.

Through this journey, I have come to understand that abundance is not just about material wealth; it is about living a life that is rich in love, joy, purpose, and fulfilment. It is about being grateful and always recognizing the infinite possibilities that life offers and embracing them with an open heart and an expanded mind. By shifting my negative self-narratives and cultivating an abundance mindset, I have been able to transform my life in ways I never thought possible.

Today, I no longer see myself as a product of scarcity but as a creator of success and abundance. I am proud of the journey I have undertaken and the person I have become. My story is no longer one of struggle and lack, but of growth, empowerment, and endless possibilities. And as I continue on this journey, I am committed to helping others do the same, empowering them to rewrite their own narratives and embrace the abundance that life has to offer.

What's Your Relationship with Language?

Language is a powerful tool. Its power lies in its ability to shape thoughts, behaviours, and interactions, fostering social connection and facilitating cooperation. It's integral to our human experience, playing an important role in shaping our identities, our culture, and the world we live in.

Your relationship with language, in the context of this book, refers to the words that you choose to describe your past experiences, your interactions, and more importantly the emotions attached to them. A lot of the words we use when conveying our stories are driven by our subconscious thoughts. The vocabulary that we use to express ourselves and understand the world around us can either be positive or negative. Both are influenced greatly by how we experience things in our lives, especially from childhood. If you were told as a child that you will never amount to anything if you do not finish school, you will likely equate academic achievement to success and if indeed you did not finish school, then you will most likely consider yourself a failure in life for not having done so. As a result, you find yourself undermining all your other successes thinking 'yes this is good, but I am not good enough'.

When we have a positive relationship with language, our self-narratives are more empowering and uplifting. We use words that affirm our strengths, achievements, and aspirations that nurture self-confidence and resilience. Positive language can help us frame problems as opportunities for growth, motivating us to overcome obstacles and pursue our goals. Our self-narrative might include phrases like 'I am capable' or 'I am resilient'; these types of statements reinforce a sense of self-efficacy and optimism in ourselves.

The Dangers of Misplaced Humility

It's not surprising that we almost always cringe at the thought of describing ourselves in a positive way and patting ourselves on the back especially when speaking to others. For most of us this all goes back to our upbringing. We all have been taught, at one point or another, to be humble as part of our so-called values formation. There is nothing wrong with this, except for the fact that it deprived us of the ability to be appreciative of ourselves when we actually did something worthy of praise. We therefore grew up with the notion that if we were not being humble, then we must be arrogant or conceited. There seems to be no middle ground, there is just this huge gap that most of us don't know how to fill, and we wonder why we feel so inadequate and incomplete. We often find ourselves at the mercy of some authority figure, a parent, a boss, a partner, a friend, or our children to heap praise on us to feel valued and celebrated for our accomplishments. I think not having the language to be able to appreciate and celebrate our own successes is brutal. This is misplaced humility, and it is detrimental to our well-being.

Humility is considered misplaced when it brings about undesirable outcomes or is used in scenarios where self-confidence, decisiveness, and good judgment would be more appropriate. Here are some examples of where humility might be misplaced:

1. **Inadequate self-assessment**
   When one consistently downplays their capabilities and contributions at work for example, they could miss out on their due recognition or opportunities they deserve to advance in their career. This can lead to job dissatisfaction

and being undervalued and taken advantage of by others who might exploit their talents.

2. **Avoidance of necessary conflict**
   Excessive humility usually leads to passive behaviour. In cases where one needs to stand up for themselves to protect their rights and beliefs, taking a passive stance could result in tolerating unfair treatment or allowing others to abuse and manipulate them.

3. **Enabling incompetence**
   If a person in a leadership role for instance is overly humble and minimizes their role in the spirit of camaraderie, they might hold back in providing necessary feedback or deliver sanctions to their staff when wrongdoings are committed. This can enable offenses and unethical behaviour to continue unchecked and poison the culture well, so to speak.

4. **Abandoning personal well-being**
   Prioritizing others' needs is a selfless act that we can all use a little of, but when done excessively it can result in burnout, resentment, or diminished self-worth. Abandoning our own well-being can lead to compassion fatigue, this happens when we forget to replenish ourselves and tend to our needs in a healthy way. As the old adage goes, you can never pour from an empty cup.

5. **Undermining trust and credibility**
   Too much humility in a leader for example can oftentimes erode people's confidence in a person's ability to take charge and can make subordinates feel uncertain about the direction of the team. It may also cause them to doubt the capabilities of an overly humble leader and fail to inspire confidence and trust especially when it comes to managing crises and critical situations.

6. **Weakened self-advocacy**
   In negotiations, whether it's for a contract or in personal relationships, misplaced humility can cause someone to settle for less than they need or deserve. This ultimately affects their long-term success and self-fulfilment.

7. **Misconstrued intentions**
   Excessive humility can sometimes come across as false modesty leading others to misread a person's intentions or authenticity.

To sum up, although humility for the most part is a positive trait, it can also prevent us from claiming our worth, solve issues that require forthrightness and good judgment, and more importantly achieve our goals in a self-empowered way when left unchecked and inadvertently misplaced.

Changing a Self-Narrative Without Altering One's Past

As mentioned earlier, changing our self-narratives from negative to positive ones does not mean lying about our past or history. It is simply a way of reframing our interpretation of our past experiences. This process is about shifting your perspective and the story you tell yourself about who you are and what your past means to you. Here's how you can do that:

1. **Reflect on your current self-narrative**
   You can begin by observing the stories you have been telling yourself. What recurring themes tend to come up when you talk about your past? Are they limiting or liberating, self-defeating or self-empowering? What emotions tend to come up? Is it sadness or gladness, regret or delight? Pay close attention to your body language as well. Are you hunched over or do your shoulders expand?

Do you wear a smile on your face or a furrowed brow when you talk about them?

2. **Accept your past but don't let it define you**
   Look at past events with fresh eyes. See your failures and hardships as life lessons that brought you to where you are now. View them as necessary events that have contributed to your resilience and wisdom. They have shaped you, but they do not define your whole identity. It's a part of your story, not the whole of it. And it will certainly not define your future.

3. **Focus on your strengths and accomplishments**
   However hard or bitter you think your past was, focus on the positive aspects of your journey. Place emphasis on your unique strengths that made you triumph over extreme difficulty or prevailed despite limited resources.

4. **Adopt a future-oriented narrative**
   Envision a better you. Start telling a story of who you are becoming based on your values and the characteristics that you love about yourself. Align this narrative with your aspirations and your goals to create a compelling future.

5. **Seek supportive feedback**
   Surround yourself with people who see your potential. Oftentimes, others see strengths in us that we do not realize we have. External validation can help reshape your story.

6. **Be gentle with yourself**
   Accord yourself the same compassion you would a friend if they make mistakes or have regrets. Acknowledge that everyone makes mistakes and has flaws. Just remember that growth comes from learning from our mistakes and

that dwelling on past errors and living in regret never benefitted anyone.

These strategies can help you create a more empowering and accurate story that can help you reshape your self-narrative. It can eliminate the feelings of blame and shame that typically accompanies difficult experiences. This allows you to honour the past but it does not dictate your future, and it paints a positive picture of who you are now and who you are becoming.

Overall, our relationship with language profoundly influences our self-perception and emotional well-being. Positive narratives can empower us to overcome challenges and achieve our potential, while negative narratives can undermine our confidence and hinder our progress. Recognizing the power of language in shaping our self-narratives allows us to cultivate a more positive and empowering relationship with ourselves and with the world.

Here are a hundred positive narratives that you can use in your life starting today. Find two or three that resonate the most with you and make them your own personal affirmation statements, a mantra if you may.

1. *I have the ability to reach my dreams through dedication and persistence.*
2. *My distinctive talents shape my journey and help me achieve my ambitions.*
3. *I turn challenges into stepping stones for personal growth.*
4. *I honour my past achievements while eagerly anticipating my future.*
5. *My creative mind allows me to solve problems in innovative ways.*
6. *I am adaptable and rise above any difficulty that comes my way.*
7. *My enthusiasm fuels me to bring out the best in every situation.*
8. *My setbacks do not define me; my perseverance and effort do.*
9. *I am constantly evolving, embracing every new version of myself.*
10. *I have faith in my abilities and confidence in my potential.*

11. *I am open to receiving the success, love, and happiness I deserve.*
12. *My focus and dedication pave the way for meaningful outcomes.*
13. *I am grateful for the resilience that challenges have helped me build.*
14. *I hold the power to design a fulfilling and purposeful life.*
15. *My compassion extends to myself and those around me, creating positive connections.*
16. *Each new day is an opportunity to approach life with excitement and curiosity.*
17. *My abilities empower me to face life's tasks with confidence.*
18. *I cherish my achievements, no matter their size, as each step matters.*
19. *I take pride in the dedication and hard work that have led to my accomplishments.*
20. *Change is a catalyst for personal transformation, and I embrace it fully.*
21. *I bring value to the lives of those around me, enhancing our shared experiences.*
22. *I rely on my inner wisdom to guide me through life's decisions.*
23. *New opportunities and adventures enrich my life, and I welcome them.*
24. *The support I receive strengthens my resolve to succeed and grow.*
25. *I uplift and encourage those around me with my optimism and determination.*
26. *A positive outlook attracts favourable results into my life.*
27. *I am equipped to handle life's surprises with resilience and grace.*
28. *My uniqueness is a source of pride, and I celebrate what sets me apart.*
29. *I acknowledge my journey and give myself credit for all I've achieved.*
30. *I face every challenge with courage and turn obstacles into opportunities.*
31. *I embrace lifelong learning, allowing myself to grow with each experience.*
32. *Taking time for myself is essential, and I deserve moments of joy and relaxation.*

33. *I approach problems with an innovative mindset and find creative solutions.*
34. *I am continually improving, and I appreciate the progress I make every day.*
35. *I am thankful for the countless opportunities to learn, grow, and thrive.*
36. *I hold the power to influence my future with the choices I make today.*
37. *My persistence and determination are the keys to unlocking my potential.*
38. *I am fully deserving of realizing my dreams and aspirations.*
39. *I radiate positivity, bringing light into every situation I encounter.*
40. *I value the person I've become and look forward to who I'm still becoming.*
41. *I nurture my strengths while showing kindness as I work on my challenges.*
42. *I have people in my life who encourage me to be the best version of myself.*
43. *Passion and purpose fuel every step I take toward my goals.*
44. *My individuality adds unique value to every situation I am part of.*
45. *I am grateful for my gifts and how they allow me to make a difference in others' lives.*
46. *I have the ability to create long-lasting, meaningful change in my world.*
47. *I trust my instincts to lead me toward a balanced, fulfilling life.*
48. *I am fully capable of reaching any goal I set for myself.*
49. *The pursuit of my dreams brings joy and fulfilment to my life.*
50. *I am worthy of the success and happiness that flow into my life.*
51. *I create a positive impact on those around me through my actions and words.*
52. *I celebrate the journey of self-discovery and embrace who I am becoming.*
53. *I rise to challenges with strength and grace, finding solutions where others see problems.*

54. *Growth comes with every new experience I take on, and I welcome them all.*
55. *I am thankful for the relationships in my life that give me strength and comfort.*
56. *I embody positivity, becoming a role model for those around me.*
57. *I trust life's process, knowing that each step takes me closer to where I need to be.*
58. *I have the power to make a difference, both in my life and in the world around me.*
59. *I celebrate my journey, knowing that progress, no matter how small, is an achievement.*
60. *I am worthy of all the wonderful things the universe has to offer.*
61. *My curiosity about the world around me leads me to new possibilities.*
62. *I admire my resilience and the courage I show when facing challenges.*
63. *I appreciate my unique skills, knowing they allow me to navigate life creatively.*
64. *Hard work and determination empower me to achieve incredible things.*
65. *I am constantly expanding my potential and transforming into a better version of myself.*
66. *My life is filled with opportunities for success, and I take full advantage of them.*
67. *I stand out by embracing the qualities that make me different from others.*
68. *I trust my ability to navigate life's challenges with clarity and wisdom.*
69. *I am worthy of receiving love, respect, and kindness from others.*
70. *I acknowledge and appreciate the positive experiences in my life.*
71. *I inspire strength within myself and others through my actions and mindset.*
72. *I have faith in my journey and trust the path I'm on.*
73. *My progress toward my goals gives me a sense of fulfilment and pride.*

74. *I am fully dedicated to my personal growth and improvement.*
75. *The encouragement from those around me helps fuel my determination to succeed.*
76. *I have the power to create the changes I want to see in my life.*
77. *I honour my hard work and the accomplishments it has brought into my life.*
78. *I am open to receiving the success and happiness that life brings my way.*
79. *New experiences and opportunities enrich my life, and I look forward to them.*
80. *My ability to face challenges head-on gives me the courage to keep moving forward.*
81. *The lessons I've learned shape me into a wiser, stronger individual.*
82. *I strive to create harmony and balance in every area of my life.*
83. *I make a positive difference in the world around me.*
84. *I am open to receiving all the love and joy life offers.*
85. *My belief in myself brings about positive outcomes and success.*
86. *I appreciate the abundance that surrounds me and welcome more into my life.*
87. *I take pride in the person I've become and the progress I continue to make.*
88. *My life is fuelled by passion and guided by a strong sense of purpose.*
89. *I deserve all the good that comes into my life, and I welcome it fully.*
90. *I embrace new opportunities with excitement and an open mind.*
91. *My positivity and strength create a ripple effect, impacting others.*
92. *I have full confidence in my ability to make my dreams a reality.*
93. *The love and support from those around me fill me with gratitude.*
94. *My resilience empowers me to persevere through even the toughest challenges.*

95. *I am deserving of a life filled with happiness, fulfilment, and success.*
96. *My unique perspective and skills allow me to make valuable contributions.*
97. *I have the power to create lasting change in the world and my own life.*
98. *Every new experience brings me closer to my best self, and I welcome that growth.*
99. *I am grateful for how far I've come and excited for the person I'm still becoming.*
100. *I have confidence in my ability to create a life filled with joy, success, and purpose.*

Chapter 4 Summary: The Practice of Positive Self-Narratives

In this chapter, we uncovered the transformative power of the stories we tell ourselves. Our self-narratives shape how we see our past, experience the present, and envision the future. By reframing these stories, we can shift from being passive victims of circumstance to active creators of our destiny. The practice of positive self-narratives allows us to rewrite limiting beliefs, embrace a mindset of abundance, and cultivate a life filled with meaning, resilience, and endless possibilities.

5 Key Takeaways

1. **The power of self-narratives**
   - The stories we tell ourselves determine how we view our lives and shape our decisions.
   - By understanding the language that we use to describe our experiences, we gain the ability to rewrite disempowering narratives into ones that are constructive and empowering.

2. **Thriving vs. surviving**
    - Survivors focus on endurance and just getting past hardships. Thrivers on the other hand seek growth, meaning, and joy even amidst challenges.
    - The key to thriving lies in shifting thought patterns, embracing curiosity, and adopting a mindset of transformation over mere survival.

3. **Reframing the past without denying it**
    - Changing your self-narrative doesn't mean altering history; it's about interpreting your experiences in a way that empowers rather than limits you.
    - Accepting your past while focusing on the strengths, lessons, and resilience it gave you allows you to transform obstacles into stepping stones to success.
4. **Language shapes your reality**
    - The words you use to describe yourself and your circumstances directly impact your mindset and emotional well-being.
    - Positive self-narratives foster confidence, resilience, and a sense of possibility, while negative narratives reinforce fear, self-doubt, and limitation.

5. **Breaking free from scarcity to embrace abundance**
    - A scarcity mindset focuses on lack and limitations, keeping you stuck in a cycle of self-sabotage and struggle.
    - An abundance mindset opens up opportunities, encourages long-term vision, and fosters growth by focusing on what is possible and within reach.

My Final Thoughts

Practicing positive self-narratives is a powerful tool for reshaping your life. By choosing to tell stories that highlight your strengths, embrace your potential, and focus on abundance, you can transform how you view yourself and your circumstances. This practice empowers you to move from survival to thriving, helping you create a life that reflects your true worth, aspirations, and limitless possibilities.

CHAPTER 5

Practice Positive Rituals

> *'Habits. It's where goals go to die.'*
>
> —Unknown

Rituals Are Habits with Intention

Rituals are important for us human beings because we thrive in safety and predictability. Our brains need that. Rituals are the little things we do on a daily basis that produce results, in other words, our habits—it's what we do or don't do; what we say or don't say; what we eat or don't eat—that cause us to be who and where we are now in our life. Repeated actions create patterns that form our reality and therefore our life. One of the most critical aspects of achieving any goal is understanding the role that habits play.

As mentioned in this chapter's epigraph, habits are often where goals go to die. This happens when people set ambitious goals but fail to establish the daily rigors to support them. Habits are the small, repeated actions that compound over time to create significant change. Habits, especially micro habits, are the force that keeps progress moving forward and overcome obstacles on the path to success. They are the secret ingredients that hold the most powerful punch when it comes to making change sustainable and goals achievable. It's like adding a pinch of salt to a recipe; without those tiny crystals our cooking would not reach its delicious potential.

While our goals provide an overarching direction, our micro habits create the stable foundation needed to achieve them and if our routines are not congruent with our goals, reaching them will always be very difficult. Without the right rituals, even the most modest of goals will fall apart. It does not matter how well-intended our goals are, if we keep doing the same old things that got us here, we will never get further than here. The actions that we choose to employ against our desired goals provide the solid and fertile ground that will keep us rooted in our vision so we can see that goal through to the end no matter the obstacles.

Rituals Build Momentum

Momentum is the invisible force behind lasting change. Change is a gradual process that takes patience and perseverance, and this doesn't come from giant leaps but from stacking small, consistent actions. This is where the idea of rituals ties back into the process of personal evolution. If you want to create lasting change, it's important to take it one small step at a time. Too often, people get discouraged by the enormity of their goals, thinking they need to make massive shifts overnight to get started on the right foot. But the reality is that it is the small, manageable changes compounding over time that propel us to the right trajectory for larger transformations.

This principle applies to all areas of life. Whether your goal is to advance in your career, improve your relationships, or cultivate a healthier lifestyle, the key is to start small. Identify one ritual that aligns with your goal and incorporate it into your daily routine. Likewise, identify one that does not align and stop doing that one thing. With consistency, what once felt difficult becomes more manageable. Over time, that small action will build strength and velocity, and before you know it, you'll be well on your way to creating the future you have envisioned.

How Rituals Shape Our Reality

Rituals, whether we are aware of them or not, play a central role in determining our experience of the present circumstances. If you've ever wondered how you got to this point in your life—whether it's your career, relationships, or your overall state of health—the answer lies in the small, repeated actions you've been engaging in and stacking up over time.

So how do you create habits that actually help you achieve your goals? The key lies in making the habit-building process as simple and consistent as possible. For example, at work, your current career trajectory is likely not the result of big dramatic one-time efforts, but rather through consistent small, reliable, and measurable actions that demonstrated your expertise and dependability in the workplace, e.g. always coming in on time for meetings, spending a few extra minutes each week to teach a coworker a new skill or learn a new skill yourself, or following a daily to-do list to organize your tasks more efficiently and effectively. These micro habits, however small, compound over time and create noticeable improvements by your superiors in your productivity, your reliability and leadership potential.

In personal relationships, the strength of your connections often hinges on micro habits to ensure its quality and longevity. Small habits like a quick call or text to check in with family members, actively listening during conversations, or giving daily words of affirmation can go a long way in building a deep sense of connectedness to each other. These tiny but consistent actions build trust and intimacy that nurture relationships for years and years to come.

When it comes to your physical or psychological well-being, it's not the big actions like starting an intense fitness regimen or sitting in a one-hour meditation session right away that make the difference. It's the micro habits like practicing two minutes of deep breathing in the morning, taking frequent sips of water throughout the day, or taking five-minute stretch breaks at your desk every two hours. These small manageable habits, when done daily, compound over time, leading to significant improvements in your physical and mental health.

It might seem like these habits are insignificant on their own, but when incorporated in your daily life consistently, like brushing your teeth or combing your hair, they stack up and shape the outcomes in your career, relationships, and overall well-being in a very positive way.

For example, consider a person who sets the goal of losing weight and becoming healthier. This is a sensible and worthwhile goal, but without the supporting habits—like exercising regularly, eating nutritious foods, and getting enough sleep—it's unlikely to be achieved. Many people fall into the trap of setting huge goals without implementing the regimen required to achieve them. Let's break down our examples a bit further.

If you want to build a habit of exercising regularly, the secret is in establishing micro habits. You may start by laying out your shoes, shirt, and sweatpants the night before so you can quickly put them on when you wake up in the morning. This eliminates the mental load of having to decide what to wear on your run and gets you out the door quickly. It only takes a small amount of effort at the end of the day and yet it makes a huge difference in the early mornings when you're dealing with poor decision-making on account of sleepiness, which typically ends up with you giving up before you even started.

Same goes for your food choices, don't just cut off all sugar and carbs in one go, this is a recipe for disaster. If you always have sweet coffee and pancakes for breakfast, for example, try black coffee without the sugar with your sweet pancakes for a change, or vice versa, skip the maple syrup in favour of the sweet coffee. You'll get the same kick you need in the morning but without the sugar overload. Remember, our bodies still need sugar, the danger is in the dose.

As for sleep, you can start to adopt good sleep hygiene by giving up screen time thirty minutes before your intended bedtime. You still get to scroll but you don't fall into the trap of doom-scrolling the night away. These tactics give you a sense of accomplishment without feeling like you've been deprived , which in turn motivates you to make more micro changes in many other ways. Stacked together over time they will result in new rituals that support your goals. Before you know it, you are well on your way to a healthier lifestyle. This is why rituals are so essential, they build the momentum necessary to support long-term change and move us toward our desired future.

How to Build Rituals That Support Your Goals

1. **Start with micro habits**
   Begin with small, simple actions that are easy to do. Micro habits make big goals feel less overwhelming and help you take that all-important first step.
   - Example: Want to start meditating? Begin with just one minute of listening to the natural rhythm of your breath everyday instead of aiming for thirty minutes of guided meditation right away.

2. **Focus on incremental changes**
   Don't try to change everything at once. Take small, gradual steps in the right direction so your mind and body can adjust naturally. Small changes add up over time and are much easier to stick with.
   - Example: If you want to eat healthier, start by adding a serving of vegetables to your meals rather than overhauling your entire diet at once.

3. **Adopt change-friendly practices**
   Set yourself up for success by making changes easier. Remove obstacles, create reminders, and build routines that support your goals. The easier you make it, the more likely you'll follow through.
   - Example: If your goal is to work out in the morning, set out your workout clothes, sneakers, and water bottle the night before, so everything is ready to go for you in the morning.

4. **Build momentum through small wins**
   Celebrate your little victories. Small wins keep you motivated, show that your efforts are paying off, and help you stay on track. They make the journey enjoyable and rewarding.
   - Example: If you successfully drink a glass of water first thing every morning for a week, treat yourself to a new water bottle as a reward.

5. **Stack your micro habits**
   Combine small habits into routines. When one habit becomes automatic, link it to another. Over time, these stacked habits create powerful daily rituals that make progress effortless.
   - Example: If you already prepare your morning coffee, use the time it brews to jot down three things you're grateful for, creating a gratitude practice alongside your existing routine.

6. **Focus on progress, not perfection**
   It's okay to mess up. What matters is that you're moving forward. Celebrate every bit of progress and keep going, even if it's not perfect.
   - Example: If you miss a workout one day, don't beat yourself up. Just get back on track the next day and keep going.

7. **Enjoy the journey to long-term change**
   Change takes time, so you might as well find joy in the process instead of dreading it. Treat challenges as opportunities to grow and appreciate how far you've come. Loving the journey makes success even sweeter.
   - Example: As you build your new morning routine, take a moment to enjoy the quiet time you've carved out for yourself instead of obsessing on the end goal.

The Future Is Not a Place to Go to, it's a Place to Come From

This idea, made popular by the political theorist John Schaar, shifts our understanding of the future from something that happens to us, to something we actively create. This isn't just a mindset shift; it's the fundamental truth of how life unfolds, *and it is particularly evident for individuals who are not oppressed and have a certain degree of autonomy and freedom to shape their circumstances.* This is an important distinction to keep in mind as we flesh out this idea.

The future is not something distant or separate from us; it is in fact being shaped by our decisions, actions, thoughts and even our emotions in the present moment. This is a reality of life. The future we will experience is a result of what we are doing right now, it is not some predestined circumstance we have no influence over. The best part? The future arrives one day at a time, giving us the opportunity to shape it with the actions we take today. By integrating positive rituals into our daily lives, we have the power to design the future we want, one day, one step, and one small habit at a time.

We often think of the future as something in the far beyond, a set destination that we will get to someday. We might even think that it was simply dealt to us by some unforeseen hand, and we have no control over it. But in reality, we are the creators of our future through the choices that we make and the actions that we take to support those choices. It doesn't just happen to us—it is in fact a direct outcome of how we approach our present lives. For instance, if you want to better your financial situation in the future, it won't happen by waiting for luck or external circumstances to change. Instead, it happens because of the small, good financial habits you practice today, like saving, budgeting, and investing.

This truth applies to all areas of life. The relationships you will have in the future are shaped by the way you treat yourself and other people today. When you are kind and loving to yourself and others, you will attract a kind and loving equal. Your future health is being determined by the foods you eat, the exercise you do, and how you manage stress in your life now. Every small action compounds over time, eventually becoming the envisioned future you will experience.

The future is not an abstract concept that is 'out there'. It is something we create, something that is constructed into being through our daily actions and decisions. By being aware of this reality, we understand that we have far more control over our future than we might think. The seeds we plant today grow into the life we will live tomorrow. It's an undeniable truth that the future is constantly coming from who we are being in the present.

While this notion highlights our power in shaping the future through our present actions, as mentioned earlier, there are exceptions where the future is truly not within our control. Here are such exceptions:

- **Death**: While we can influence many aspects of our future, death is inevitable and largely beyond our control. We can take steps to live healthily, but ultimately, the reality of mortality transcends personal agency.
- **Natural disasters**: Events we refer to as acts of God—like earthquakes, hurricanes, or tsunamis—are unpredictable and uncontrollable. While we can prepare for and mitigate risks, the occurrence of such natural events and

their timing are outside the scope of human influence, often altering the future without warning.

- **Pandemics and widespread health crises**: As seen with events like the COVID-19 pandemic, global health crises can rapidly alter the course of the future for individuals, communities, and entire countries. These events limit personal control and can reshape economies, health systems, and social structures.
- **Political instability, war, acts of violence or terrorism**: In regions affected by political upheaval, war, authoritarian regimes, or terrorism, people's futures are strongly dictated by external forces, such as government policies, conflicts, or human rights violations, which can severely restrict personal agency and opportunities for change.
- **Global economic crises**: Events like recessions, inflation, or global financial collapses are largely uncontrollable by individuals. These crises can drastically alter people's lives and futures, affecting jobs, savings, and opportunities in ways that are impossible to fully predict or control.

Having said that, one might argue still that despite the significant external factors that can limit control over the future, individuals can still take small, consistent actions—micro habits—to regain some sense of volition and pursue a better future. Here are some practical examples of how micro habits might apply to each of the exceptions I mentioned:

- **Death**: While death is inevitable, cultivating a daily habit of gratitude can help shift focus to the present and enhance life's quality. For example, writing down three things you're grateful for every day, despite your grief, can help you live more meaningfully in the present moment.
- **Natural disasters**: While uncontrollable, developing a micro habit of preparation can minimize the negative

impacts of natural disasters. A simple habit could be dedicating five minutes a week to reviewing or updating an emergency kit or evacuation plan, increasing preparedness and reducing anxiety.

- **Pandemics and widespread health crises**: Amid health crises, a micro habit of daily hygiene practices, such as washing hands regularly or disinfecting high-touch surfaces, can help reduce exposure risks and promote a sense of control.
- **Political instability, war, acts of violence or terrorism**: In situations where people have little control over their political environment and overall safety, a micro habit of reaching out to the community for connection can provide support. Taking a minute each day to check in with friends, family, or neighbours can strengthen resilience and foster a network of mutual aid.
- **Global economic crises**: During economic downturns, financial habits like saving small amounts can make a difference. Even saving a few dollars a week can build up over time and provide a sense of security, which can be helpful during crises.

While these micro habits may not solve the larger issues, they offer small ways for individuals to regain some control over their lives and move toward a better future despite external limitations. These habits focus on manageable actions that, over time, can make a significant impact on personal well-being.

Movement Is the Antidote to Stress

One of the easiest and most powerful rituals you can incorporate into your life is movement. Our bodies are designed to move, and if we don't, stress accumulates in our physical body and lives in our cells. Unbeknownst to many, stress is fundamentally a physiological event rather than just a mental or emotional experience. It all begins in the body as a reaction to perceived threats, whether they are physical, emotional, or psychological. While many people think of stress as something that happens in their minds—like anxiety, worry, or being overwhelmed—it's actually rooted in the body's natural 'fight, flight, or freeze' response. This means that you can't simply 'think your way out' of stress.

In the book *Burnout: The Secret to Unlocking the Stress Cycle* by Emily and Amelia Nagoski, the authors explain that physical movement is one of the most effective ways to complete the 'stress cycle' and release built-up tension in the body. This cycle involves releasing stress hormones like adrenaline and cortisol out of the body. To fully resolve stress, the body needs to physically discharge the stress hormones that get triggered by our brains whenever we encounter stressful situations. Noradrenaline is released in the heart to increase heart rate, amplify contractions, and increase blood pressure to prepare the body for fast action in response to a threat. Adrenaline is released in the muscles to increase blood flow to deliver more oxygen and nutrients to fuel increased muscle activity when you need to run away or fight off a perceived threat. Cortisol, the most notorious of them all, is a longer-lasting stress hormone that increases glucose availability in the body and provides sustained energy to muscles during prolonged stress or physical activity.

So, as you can imagine, if the stress cycle is left incomplete and the body is unable to utilize these hormones according to what they were intended for—which is active physical activity to fight or flee—all of this gets trapped in the cells. Meanwhile, the heart awaits action and continues to pump increasing pressure in the circulatory system, digestion slows down drastically, and the muscles remain strained and elongated to prepare for a sprint, all to no avail. Stress remains unresolved until we literally act on it. Movement is what signals our bodies that the danger has passed.

Without this, all those hormones will wreak havoc in our system over time. This ultimately results in diseases like high blood pressure, gastric problems, diabetes, muscle pain, cancer, and a host of other maladies we know as chronic illnesses. They are called chronic because they develop over time.

Short-term stress is not the issue here, in fact short-term stress is crucial for our survival as a species. This is what keeps us safe by preparing the body to confront danger (fight) or escape from it (flight). In its original evolutionary context, stress was essential for the survival of early humans and remains a key component of how we respond to danger today. While stress is a survival mechanism that allows us to adapt to threatening conditions, it becomes harmful when prolonged or chronic. Movement to release stress doesn't have to be high intensity or time-consuming to be effective. With stress being so persistent in our modern lives, movement just needs to be as consistent too.

The key takeaway is that stress is not just a mental event that can be solved through cognitive efforts. It is an embodied experience that requires a physical solution—whether through movement, relaxation techniques, or other forms of physical activity—to release the pent-up stress and restore balance to the body. By treating stress as a physiological process, you can avoid being stuck in a constant state of tension, prevent burnout, and promote long-term health.

Get Your DOSE and Feel Good

DOSE is an acronym that stands for dopamine, oxytocin, serotonin, and endorphins. These are four vital hormones and neurotransmitters responsible for up-regulating mood, feelings of happiness, and other positive emotions. These chemicals play a critical role in governing emotions, motivation, and stress. These hormones are often referred to as the 'feel-good' hormones. Here's why:

- **Dopamine** is known as the 'reward' hormone. It is released when we accomplish something, receive praise, or feel pleasure. It is what fuels motivation and reinforces behaviour by creating a sense of satisfaction and achievement.
- **Oxytocin** is often called the 'love' or 'bonding' hormone. Oxytocin is released when we are interacting with other people, during physical touch, and when we are engaged in bonding experiences such as hugging, holding hands, or kissing. This hormone allows us to form close relationships and deep connections with others. It promotes feelings of trust, safety, and emotional intimacy.
- **Serotonin** is the hormone most often linked to emotional regulation. It helps stabilize mood, anxiety, and is associated with feelings of calm and contentment. It also plays a role in sleep and appetite control.
- **Endorphins** are the body's natural painkillers. This naturally occurs during exercise, when we're experiencing laughter, or when we are engaging in enjoyable experiences like singing, dancing and other stimulating hobbies. Endorphins reduce pain and trigger elevated emotions, sometimes referred to as a 'runner's high'.

By consistently engaging in activities that naturally boost these hormones—like exercise, social connection, accomplishing tasks big or small, as well as doing acts of kindness like gratitude and generosity—we can close the loop of the stress cycle more effectively and increase our feelings of well-being.

The Role of Gratitude and Generosity in Cultivating Positive Rituals

In addition to movement, two other powerful rituals that can greatly enhance our well-being are gratitude and generosity.

Grounding ourselves in the daily practice of these values greatly shifts our focus from what's lacking in our life to what's abundant. It's a simple but powerful way to rewire our brains for positivity and infinite possibilities. According to research, individuals who regularly practice gratitude and generosity experience higher levels of happiness and lower levels of depression and stress.

One easy way to incorporate gratitude into our daily routine is by keeping a gratitude journal. Each morning or evening, write down three things we are grateful for. These don't have to be big or profound—sometimes the smallest things, like a warm cup of coffee or a bright sunny day, can have the greatest impact. Over time, this practice trains our brain to focus on the positive aspects of life, enhancing our overall sense that life is good.

Generosity, too, is a powerful ritual that doesn't have to involve grand gestures or material wealth. This is not about acts of giving that changes the world or a person's life single handedly in one fell swoop. This is about making a contribution with whatever resources that are available to us. We can be generous with our time, our knowledge, and especially our assumptions. For example, we can volunteer our time to help a friend, offer our expertise to a classmate or colleague, or give someone the benefit of the doubt in a difficult situation. Acts of generosity or contribution, no matter how small, have been shown to increase life satisfaction and an uplifting sense of being part of the solution rather than the problem.

Generosity also fosters a sense of connection with others, which is essential for emotional well-being. Humans are social creatures, and our well-being is deeply interconnected with our relationships. By practicing generosity, we not only improve our own well-being but also contribute to the well-being of others, creating a ripple effect of good feelings and positivity.

Creating the Future Through Rituals

At the heart of all these rituals—movement, gratitude, generosity, and building positive habits—is the idea that the future is not something that happens to us. It's something we create every day with our actions. As Peter Drucker said, 'The best way to predict the future is to create it.' Each day presents an opportunity to shape the future we want. By focusing on small, manageable actions and turning them into consistent rituals, we actively create the future rather than wait for it to happen. This approach gives us a sense of agency and control over our lives. Instead of being passive recipients of whatever the future holds, we become active participants in shaping it.

In the end, the future is not a destination waiting for us. It's something we create every day through the choices we make, the actions we take, and the rituals we embrace. So, what rituals will you start today to create the future you desire?

Chapter 5 Summary: Practice Positive Rituals

In this chapter, we delved into the importance of small, consistent actions that anchor our intentions and build the momentum we need to achieve meaningful and lasting outcomes. Rituals are the building blocks of transformation, shaping how we approach goals, and create lasting change.

5 Key Takeaways

1. **Rituals are habits with intention**
   Rituals are more than just habits; they are clear, intentional actions that align with our values which turn our visions into

realities. They provide stability, give a sense of predictability, and create a foundation for sustainable progress towards our goals. Without rituals, even the most well-thought-out goals can falter.

2. **Big momentum comes from small actions**
   Lasting change isn't about grand gestures but about small steps taken consistently over time. These micro habits accumulate, creating an unstoppable force that drives meaningful transformation. Whether it's a daily two-minute meditation or preparing tomorrow's to-do list today, small efforts add up and compound into noticeable and significant results.

3. **Rituals reflect and shape our reality**
   The life we experience is determined by the actions we take repeatedly. Whether in health, relationships, or career, rituals reflect our priorities and determine our outcomes. Positive rituals, like expressing daily gratitude for example, create a reality aligned with our aspirations.

4. **Movement, gratitude, and generosity fuel positive change**
   Incorporating movement into our daily routines helps release stress and boosts physical and mental well-being. Gratitude shifts our focus from what's missing to what's abundant, while generosity fosters connection and meaning. Together, these rituals enrich both our inner and outer lives.

5. **The future is not a destination**
   Our future isn't a pre-determined place or event that passively awaits us down the road. It's an experience of life that we actively create in the here and now. Each decision, intentional act we perform, or choice we make now contributes to the life we will experience tomorrow. Consistency in these actions ensures that we aren't merely reacting to life but purposefully creating it.

My Final Thoughts

By adopting positive rituals, we unlock our potential to live with intention, momentum, and conviction. These seemingly small but profoundly impactful actions transform our visions and aspirations into reality, empowering us to actively craft the future we not only envision but yearn for with every fibre of our being.

CHAPTER 6

Practice Mindfulness and Meditation

> *'The goal of meditation is not to be good at meditating, it's to be good at life.'*
>
> —Unknown

A Journey from Mystical to Practical

Over the years, mindfulness and meditation have become second nature in my daily life, a rhythm as natural as breathing almost. In my experience, their impact has been so profound that it has reshaped nearly every aspect of my being. From the way I approach challenges with a sense of calm and curiosity instead of panic, to how I experience moments of joy with deeper presence and gratitude, these practices have become the foundation of my mental, emotional, physical and spiritual resilience. They have redefined how I connect with others, allowing me to listen and respond with greater empathy and understanding. Even my relationship with myself has shifted; mindfulness has taught me self-compassion and the value of embracing my imperfections. These practices have not only carried me through daily stresses but have also been a cornerstone of my healing journey, offering acceptance, belief, and surrender during times of profound uncertainty.

What began for me as cool, mystical practices to manage stress have evolved into the unshakable foundation of my path to total and complete healing, especially after receiving a life-changing cancer diagnosis. At first, they were just intriguing rituals, ones I dabbled in out of curiosity or turned to as an occasional escape from the chaos of work and life. I was one of those rare individuals in my circle who genuinely enjoyed the quiet introspection they provided, even when others might have dismissed them as 'too woowoo'. But as I continued to explore and embrace them, mindfulness and meditation revealed themselves to be so much more. Not only are they practical, but they are also transformative, and ultimately, life-sustaining.

In time, these practices became not just rituals but indispensable ways of being for me. Interestingly enough, neuroscience supports what I've come to experience firsthand: enhanced focus, emotional regulation, resilience, and a sense of inner knowing that things will turn out fine in the end. All this and more through the incredible power of neuroplasticity.

I've personally experienced how mindfulness soothes the nervous system, regulates feelings of stress and overwhelm, and delivers a sound sense of well-being, even amidst my most overwhelming physical challenges. These practices have allowed me to connect with the energy centres within my body, bringing forth a harmonious flow of energy that often felt elusive in the face of illness.

Most strikingly, I've witnessed the profound effects of heart–brain coherence, where mindful awareness of positive thoughts intentionally paired with positive emotions brings a remarkable sense of wholeness. This synchrony has offered clarity and calm during moments of deep uncertainty, grounding me when fear and doubt threatened to take over. In my experience, mindfulness and meditation have moved far beyond mere techniques—they have become the lifeline I return to again and again, guiding me through acceptance, healing, renewal, and a more intentional way of living.

Mindfulness and meditation are powerful tools that help us slow down, become more aware of the present moment, and build a sense of lasting and inner peace. But they do more than just calm us, they actually change the brain and body in ways that can improve our overall health and well-being. This is where the science behind mindfulness and meditation really shines, showing us that these practices can help us think, feel, and live better.

Before we dive into the science, let's take a moment to understand what each of these practices really are and how one differs from the other.

Mindfulness vs. Meditation: What's the Difference?

Mindfulness and meditation are closely related, but they aren't exactly the same thing. Think of mindfulness as a way of paying attention to what's happening in the present moment, without judgment. It's something we can practice anytime—while eating, walking, or even talking to someone. When we're mindful, we're fully aware of our thoughts, feelings, and surroundings, rather than getting lost in worries about the past or future.

Meditation, on the other hand, is a more focused practice where we create time and space to sit quietly and turn our attention inward. Meditation helps us enter deeper states of awareness and calm. There are many ways to meditate, some focus on the breath, others use a mantra, and some involve visualization. Unlike mindfulness, which we can practice throughout the day, meditation usually involves setting aside a specific time to focus on stillness and inner awareness.

Simply put, mindfulness is about being present in each moment as we go about our day, while meditation is a dedicated time we set aside to focus inward and go deeper. Practicing both can help us build a stronger connection with ourselves, bringing more calm and clarity into our lives.

One of the most amazing things about mindfulness and meditation is that they can actually change the brain, a process called neuroplasticity. Neuroplasticity is the brain's ability to reshape itself based on what we focus on and repeat. Just like practicing a new skill can strengthen certain parts of the brain, meditation and mindfulness impacts key brain areas that influence focus, emotional regulation, memory, empathy, and self-awareness. It strengthens the prefrontal cortex and anterior cingulate cortex for better focus and control, reduces amygdala reactivity for lower stress, enhances hippocampus and insula activity for emotional stability and empathy, quiets the default mode network (DMN) for a calmer mind, and improves the thalamus and reticular activating system (RAS) for balanced sensory processing and alertness.

Here is a short of overview on those key brain regions that are influenced by regular meditation based on scientific studies:

1. **Prefrontal cortex – focus and self-control**
   The prefrontal cortex, located at the front of the brain, is responsible for higher-order thinking, decision-making, and self-control. Meditation strengthens this area, improving our ability to focus and enhancing self-discipline. Studies show that long-term meditators tend to have more grey matter in the prefrontal cortex, which helps with attention, impulse control, and rational thinking.

2. **Amygdala – stress response and emotional regulation**
   The amygdala, deep within the brain, is associated with emotions, particularly fear and stress. Meditation can reduce activity in the amygdala, making it less reactive to stress. Regular meditation has been shown to decrease the size and activation of the amygdala, which helps lower anxiety and stress levels. This allows people to respond to challenges with a calmer mindset.

3. **Hippocampus – memory and learning**
   The hippocampus, located in the temporal lobe, plays a vital role in memory formation and emotional regulation. Meditation has been shown to increase grey matter in

the hippocampus, improving memory and emotional stability. By supporting hippocampal growth, meditation can enhance learning, emotional resilience, and the capacity for empathy.

4. **Anterior cingulate cortex (ACC) – focus and emotional regulation**
   The ACC, located in the front part of the brain, is involved in regulating attention, emotional processing, and self-control. Meditation strengthens the ACC, helping us stay focused, reduce impulsive reactions, and increase emotional stability. The ACC also plays a role in handling conflict and filtering distractions, which helps meditators sustain attention and improve cognitive control.

5. **Insula – body awareness and empathy**
   The insula, located deep within the cerebral cortex, is associated with bodily awareness and empathy. Meditation activates the insula, which enhances our awareness of bodily sensations and increases our capacity for empathy. Mindfulness practices, especially those focusing on body scans, activate the insula, helping people tune in to physical sensations, emotional states, and the feelings of others.

6. **Default mode network (DMN) – self-reflection and mind-wandering**
   The DMN is a group of brain regions active when the mind is at rest or daydreaming. It's often associated with self-referential thinking, mind-wandering, and rumination. Meditation has been shown to reduce DMN activity, quieting the 'inner chatter' and promoting a sense of presence. By reducing activity in the DMN, meditation helps prevent overthinking, reduces negative self-talk, and increases our ability to focus on the present moment.

7. **Corpus callosum – brain hemisphere communication**
   The corpus callosum, the thick band of nerve fibres connecting the left and right brain hemispheres, facilitates communication between the two sides of the brain. Meditation strengthens the corpus callosum, enhancing integration between the logical (left) and creative (right) sides. This improved integration helps meditators process information more effectively, bringing a balance between analytical and creative thinking.

8. **Thalamus – sensory processing and focus**
   The thalamus acts as the brain's 'relay station', processing sensory information and directing attention. Meditation has been shown to influence the thalamus, allowing us to filter out distractions more effectively and improving focus. When we meditate, the thalamus helps us direct our awareness inward, enhancing concentration and reducing sensory overload.

9. **Reticular activating system (RAS) – attention and arousal**
   The RAS, a network of neurons in the brainstem, regulates wakefulness and alertness. Meditation helps calm the RAS, reducing hyper-alertness, and enhancing our ability to relax. By quieting the RAS, meditation encourages a balanced state of awareness, which helps meditators become more focused and less reactive to external stimuli.

These changes show that mindfulness and meditation isn't just a thinking or relaxing exercise, it can physically reshape the brain in ways that support mental clarity, emotional resilience, and a more grounded experience of life. 'Neurons that fire together, wire together.' This means that by practicing meditation, we're not just calming the mind temporarily, we're actually making space for it to grow and build new neural pathways allowing it to become less reactive and more resilient over time. Regular meditation helps create a more balanced and integrated brain, enhancing well-being across all aspects of life.

The Role of Energy in Meditation

As we go deeper into mindfulness and meditation, we start to notice that there's more to us than just our thoughts and emotions. Underneath it all, we're made of energy—a force that powers our bodies and connects us to everything in space and time. Our bodies have several energy centres or what is popularly known in Eastern cultures as chakras, each playing a role in our physical and emotional well-being.

When our energy centres or chakras are balanced and flowing, we feel grounded, balanced, and in flow. But when they're blocked or out of sync, we might feel tense, anxious, or even physically unwell. Luckily, we can tune into these energy centres during meditation to bring them back into balance, which helps both our bodies and minds feel more connected and whole.

To work with our body's energy, we can use meditation to bring attention to these centres. Imagine the body as a series of light channels, with each energy centre along the spine glowing or buzzing with energy. These energy centres start at the base of the spine and run up to the top of the head, each one connected to different parts of our life.

The chakras are also associated with specific hormonal glands in the body. These glands play key roles in generating and regulating hormones, and their alignment with the chakras offers a fascinating perspective on the potential link between energy centres and physical well-being. Here's an overview of each chakra and its corresponding gland or hormonal centre in the body:

1. **Root chakra (Muladhara)**
    - *Location*: Base of the spine
    - *Associated gland*: Adrenal glands
    - *Function of gland*: The adrenal glands sit on top of the kidneys and produce stress hormones like cortisol and adrenaline, which are essential for survival, energy, and response to stress.

- *Connection to chakra*: The root chakra is associated with survival, stability, and grounding. The adrenal glands support these functions by regulating the body's response to stress and providing energy.

2. **Sacral chakra (Svadhisthana)**
    - *Location*: Lower abdomen, just below the navel
    - *Associated gland*: Ovaries (in females) and testes (in males)
    - *Function of glands*: The ovaries and testes produce sex hormones (oestrogen, progesterone, and testosterone) which govern reproductive health, sexual function, and fertility.
    - *Connection to chakra*: The sacral chakra is linked to productivity, creativity, sensuality, and emotions. These reproductive glands regulate sexual energy, procreation, productivity, creativity, and emotional balance.

3. **Solar plexus chakra (Manipura)**
    - *Location*: Upper abdomen, near the stomach
    - *Associated gland*: Pancreas
    - *Function of gland*: The pancreas produces insulin and glucagon, which are crucial for regulating blood sugar levels and energy.
    - *Connection to chakra*: The solar plexus chakra is connected to personal power, self-confidence, and willpower. The pancreas's role in energy regulation supports the body's vitality and self-empowerment.

4. **Heart chakra (Anahata)**
    - *Location*: Centre of the chest, near the heart
    - *Associated gland*: Thymus

- *Function of gland*: The thymus plays a role in immune system development, particularly during childhood, by helping produce T-cells that defend the body against pathogens.
- *Connection to chakra*: The heart chakra is associated with love, compassion, and healing. The thymus gland supports the body's natural healing and immune response, which aligns with the heart chakra's theme of compassion and connection.

5. **Throat chakra (Vishuddha)**
   - *Location:* Throat area
   - *Associated gland*: Thyroid and parathyroid glands
   - *Function of glands*: The thyroid regulates metabolism, energy production, and growth, while the parathyroid glands control calcium levels in the body.
   - *Connection to chakra*: The throat chakra is linked to communication, self-expression, and truth. The thyroid's role in metabolic regulation aligns with the chakra's function of enabling clear and powerful expression.

6. **Third eye chakra (Ajna)**
   - *Location*: Forehead, between the eyebrows
   - *Associated gland*: Pineal gland
   - *Function of gland*: The pineal gland produces melatonin, which regulates sleep-wake cycles, and influences circadian rhythms.
   - *Connection to chakra*: The third eye chakra is associated with intuition, wisdom, and insight. The pineal gland's role in sleep and awareness reflects this chakra's connection to inner vision and spiritual insight.

7. **Crown chakra (Sahasrara)**
    - *Location*: Top of the head
    - *Associated gland*: Pituitary gland
    - *Function of gland*: Often referred to as the 'master gland', the pituitary gland regulates other glands in the endocrine system, releasing hormones that control growth, metabolism, and body function.
    - *Connection to chakra*: The crown chakra is linked to spirituality, higher consciousness, and connection to the divine. The pituitary gland's role in regulating all other glands aligns with the crown chakra's theme of unity and enlightenment.

Table 6.1: Overview of the relationship between different chakras and glands

Chakra	Location	Associated Gland	Primary Function
Root Chakra	Base of the spine	Adrenal glands	Stress response, energy regulation
Sacral Chakra	Lower abdomen	Ovaries/ testes	Reproductive health, sexual function, creativity
Solar plexus Chakra	Upper abdomen	Pancreas	Blood sugar regulation, energy management
Heart Chakra	Centre of chest	Thymus	Immune system, healing
Throat Chakra	Throat	Thyroid/ parathyroid glands	Metabolism, growth, calcium balance
Third eye Chakra	Between eyebrows	Pineal gland	Sleep-wake cycle, circadian rhythm
Crown Chakra	Top of head	Pituitary gland	Overall endocrine regulation, spiritual connection

By understanding the connections between the chakras and glands, we can see how balancing these energy centres might influence not only emotional and spiritual health but also physical well-being. Practices that support chakra alignment, such as meditation, breathwork, and positive intention, may enhance the harmonious function of these endocrine glands, promoting balance in mind and body.

In my own experience, I sometimes feel tingling or warmth when I meditate and focus on these areas, which is usually a sign that energy is moving through the body. Whenever I feel anxious or unsafe and want to re-centre, I would focus on the energy centre at the base of my spine, breathing deeply and imagining a sense of calm. Or, if I feel disconnected from others or struggle with self-love, I would focus on the heart centre and visualize a warm light expanding in that area. By bringing attention to these energy centres, I can ease emotional and physical tension and reconnect with myself on a deeper level.

Raising Our Vibration with Positive Emotions

One of the most powerful benefits of meditation is that it can help us raise our vibration. This means that we can shift from low energy emotions, like anger or worry, to high-energy emotions, like gratitude, love, and joy. By focusing on these higher emotions in meditation, we begin to feel lighter, calmer, and more connected.

In simple terms, vibration is the natural energy or frequency at which something moves. Everything in the universe, including us, is made up of tiny particles, and these particles are always moving even if we can't see it. When we talk about vibration in a personal sense, we're talking about the energy we feel and the energy we give off.

When we're in a good mood or feeling joyful, our energy is 'high' or 'positive'. Think of this as a fast, upbeat tone like the hum of a happy energetic song. On the other hand, when we're feeling sad, angry, or stressed, our energy can feel 'low' or 'heavy', which is more like a slow, laden tone.

Just like tuning a radio, we can 'tune' ourselves into different vibrations by focusing on specific emotions and thoughts. When we intentionally raise our vibration—thinking of positive emotions like gratitude, love, or courage—we start to feel more whole and connected to the world around us. This can have a tangible effect on the people we interact with, creating a ripple of positive energy.

So, vibration is really about the energy we're experiencing inside and radiating on the outside, and by raising it, we can bring more balance, joy, and well-being into our lives.

This idea of raising our vibration is backed by science. Numerous scientific studies found that compassion meditation for example, which is a meditation focused on positive emotions like kindness, can help improve heart rate variability, a measure of heart-brain coherence. This state of balance in the heart and mind has been linked to better physical health and emotional resilience, supporting the idea that when we feel positive emotions, we bring our whole body into harmony.

Dacher Keltner, in his research on the emotion of awe, shows that people who regularly feel awe have lower levels of inflammation. We experience awe when we witness something incredible that seems almost superhuman or surreal, like when an athlete reaches a level of skill, speed, or strength that leaves us completely amazed, or witnessing the beauty of a sunset by the beach. For example, in basketball, watching a player make a buzzer-beating, game-winning shot from half-court in the last second can fill the entire stadium with awe. The skill, timing, and precision of that moment can feel almost magical, as if everything aligned perfectly.

Inflammation is often linked to stress and chronic diseases, so reducing it can have powerful effects on our health. This research suggests that when we tap into elevated emotions, even in simple ways, we are not only improving our mood but also supporting our body's natural healing processes.

Heart–Brain Coherence

When we practice meditation and focus on positive emotions, we often experience a calming, balanced state known as heart–brain coherence. Heart–brain coherence is when the rhythms of the heart and brain align, creating a harmonious flow throughout the body. This balanced state has been shown to improve mental clarity, eliminate stress, and activate the body's healing and repair mechanisms to boost physical health and even to manifest our desired intentions.

One of the most recent and profound scientific works on heart and brain coherence is by Dr Joe Dispenza. His work is grounded in the science of aligning our emotional and mental states to create harmony in our bodies. Heart–brain coherence occurs when the rhythms of our heart and brain synchronize, creating a state of homeostasis or balance that allows our mind, body, and emotions to function in unison. Dr Joe explains that when we align our attention (focused mental state) and intention (positive emotional state) through meditation, we can enter this state of coherence, which has powerful effects in our lives.

When we experience positive emotions like gratitude, love, and compassion, our heart rhythms become smoother and more stable, which in turn influences the brain's response. In this state, the heart sends signals to the brain that help us feel calm, centred, and balanced. The shift toward coherence doesn't just make us feel better emotionally, it also activates the body's natural healing and repair mechanisms, supporting new growth, resilience, mental clarity, and stress reduction. Dispenza teaches that regular practice of heart–brain coherence through meditation can create long-term changes, helping us become more grounded and growth-centred.

Positive emotions play a central role in achieving heart-brain coherence. Emotions like gratitude and love create a 'feel-good' effect because they stimulate the vagus nerve, which influences heart rate and reduces stress. When we cultivate these emotions in meditation, we are not just creating a mental state, we are also generating a physiological response that enhances communication between the heart and brain.

Studies from the HeartMath Institute, an organization dedicated to researching heart–brain coherence, has demonstrated that focusing on positive emotions leads to stable, rhythmic heart patterns that strengthen heart–brain communication. This communication is essential because the heart has its own neural network and actually sends more signals to the brain than the brain sends to the heart. When our heart rhythms are stable and coherent, these signals help regulate brain function, enhancing mental clarity and focus while promoting feelings of calm and positivity. When the heart and brain are in sync, the body activates its parasympathetic nervous system, also called the 'rest and repair' system. This activation counteracts the effects of stress by calming the nervous system, reducing the level of the stress hormone cortisol and increases DHEA, a hormone that promotes vitality and resilience. It supports the body's natural healing process by promoting antibody production and lowering inflammation, which are critical in protecting the body from illness. Coherence promotes smoother heart rhythms, which can benefit blood pressure and overall heart health, reducing the risk of stress-related conditions.

Through this meditation practice we gain greater control over our inner world, influencing how we feel, think, and respond to life. This practice isn't just about relaxation, it's a transformative approach to self-healing and personal growth. When we achieve coherence, we experience a shift in energy, mood, and perception. Our thoughts become more positive, our responses become less reactive, and we feel a greater connection to ourselves and others. Over time, this can lead to lasting changes in how we experience life, creating a foundation for deeper peace, well-being, and fulfilment.

Mindfulness and Meditation as a Skill

Mindfulness and meditation are often talked about as ways to relax or find inner peace. But these practices are more than just calming exercises that give you peace. They are skills that we can get better at over time. Like learning to play an instrument, a new sport, or cooking. The more we practice mindfulness and meditation, the more natural and effective they become.

Now that we have established the science and the effectiveness of mindfulness and meditation, let us look at how to build these skills into our everyday lives to make it practical, accessible, and rewarding.

Daily Inward Practices for Building Mindfulness

Mindfulness is all about paying attention to what's happening right here, right now. Whether we're eating, walking, or simply breathing. Practicing mindfulness regularly helps us create a habit of being fully present, which makes it easier to stay calm and balanced, especially when life gets too busy. The following suggestions are what I call 'inward mindfulness'. They are micro habits we can build that look at who we are being at any given moment in our day. The point is not to cast judgment on ourselves but to allow space to appreciate the generous present moment and break us free from the negative behaviours that we tend to get caught up in unconsciously.

One simple way to build inward mindfulness is through 'mindful breathing'. Throughout the day, we can pause and take a moment to notice how we are breathing. Is it shallow, fast, or we may even be holding it unconsciously. Taking deep breaths, focusing on the feeling of the breath moving in and out of our body, appreciating our ability to take in as much air as we need, or just simply noticing how we might slow our breath down and deepen our inhales can bring us back into being grounded. Applying this micro habit allows us to reset and bring us back to the generous present moment.

Another example is 'mindful eating'. Instead of rushing through meals or eating on autopilot, we can slow down and really experience each bite. Taste the flavours, notice the textures, and appreciate the food and the people who prepared our meals for us. Mindful eating not only helps us enjoy our meals more but also makes us more aware of how our body feels and when we're truly satisfied.

Finally, we can practice 'mindful listening' when we are in conversation with others. Instead of getting ahead and planning our response or getting distracted, we can focus fully on what the other person is saying. By being present in our conversations, we build deeper connections and show others that we're truly hearing and seeing them and that we care about what they're saying. Remember, it's not so much what we say that really matters in conversations, it's how we make the other person feel that creates a meaningful and memorable experience.

Mindful Parenting: Bringing Awareness into Family Life

Mindfulness is also a powerful tool for parenting. When we practice mindful parenting, we bring the same focus and awareness into our interactions with our children, helping us stay patient and present, even in challenging moments.

For example, instead of reacting quickly when a child is upset or acting out, we can take a deep breath and respond calmly. We might listen fully to what they're saying and give them our full attention, letting them know that we see and hear them. This mindful approach helps build a stronger, more trusting parent-child relationship.

We can also teach simple mindfulness practices to our children, practicing mindfulness together can bring a sense of calm into the home and help children feel more secure and connected. Mindful parenting practices can help cultivate a calmer, more present family environment, strengthening relationships and fostering emotional resilience in both you and your child. Incorporating these simple techniques into daily routines brings mindfulness into the heart of family life, encouraging a grounded and connected home.

Here are practical ways to bring mindfulness into parenting and deepen awareness in daily interactions with young children, teens, and young adults in the family:

With young children

1. **Listen actively**
   When your child is talking to you, make an effort to pause what you're doing and give them your full attention. Focus on their words, tone, and body language without thinking about your response. Reflect back what they're saying to show understanding and empathy, such as, 'It sounds like you're feeling frustrated because . . .'

   Active listening fosters trust, helping children feel valued and understood. This practice strengthens your connection and teaches them how to listen to others with empathy.

2. **Emotional regulation**
   In stressful moments, either for yourself or with your child, pausing and taking a few deep breaths together can make the difference between a teachable moment and a high-pitched yelling match. Model this by saying, 'Let's take three slow breaths before we talk about this.' Breathing together lowers stress and brings awareness to what is happening in the present moment, helping both you and your child approach situations with calmness and clarity.

3. **Be intentional with spending time**
   Spontaneity is good but being intentional is even better. Carve time out of your day to dedicate fifteen to thirty minutes of unstructured time with your child. Let them choose an activity, like reading a book together, drawing, or playing a game, and immerse yourself in the moment without distractions. This regular, undivided attention strengthens your bond, showing your child that they have

your full presence. It reinforces their sense of security and connection with you.

4. **Model and teach gratitude**
Each day, perhaps at bedtime or dinner, encourage each family member to share one thing they're grateful for. Start by modelling this practice, sharing your own appreciation, then inviting your child to share as well.
Gratitude fosters positive emotions, reduces stress, and helps children focus on what they already have instead of what they are missing. It's a simple practice that can shift the family's overall appreciation of life. This practice also opens up to feelings of generosity that naturally arise when we feel plentiful and abundant.

5. **Encourage 'pause and reflect' moments**
When a challenging situation arises, encourage your child to take a 'pause and reflect' moment before reacting. Guide them to ask themselves questions like, 'How do I feel right now?' and 'What would help me feel better?'
Teaching children to pause and reflect builds emotional intelligence, giving them the agency to understand and manage their feelings. This mindful pause helps them develop patience and respond with greater awareness.

For teens

Here are five additional mindfulness practices tailored to teens and young adults, helping them build awareness, resilience, and emotional intelligence in their daily lives:

1. **Encourage 'check-in' moments throughout the day**
Suggest that they take a minute in the morning, midday, and evening to ask themselves, 'How am I feeling?' and 'What do

I need right now?' They might jot down their answers in a journal or take mental notes.

Regular check-ins foster self-awareness and help them recognize and address their emotions and needs as they come up, reducing stress and promoting balanced mental health.

2. **Practice technology mindfulness**
   Encourage your teen to set boundaries with their devices by creating 'tech-free' zones or hours, especially during meals or before bed. They could also try the '5-Minute Rule': before picking up their phone, they take a mindful pause to decide if and why they need it.

   Mindful use of technology reduces the tendency to use devices for distraction or out of habit, helping teens be more intentional with their time and more present in real-life interactions.

3. **Teach the '5-4-3-2-1 grounding exercise'**
   When they feel anxious or stressed, guide them through this grounding exercise: find 5 things they can see, 4 things they can touch, 3 things they can hear, 2 things they can smell, and 1 thing they can taste.

   This technique quickly brings them back to the present moment, helping them feel grounded and less overwhelmed by stress or anxiety.

4. **Use 'setting intentions' for focus and motivation**
   Encourage them to set a daily or weekly intention, such as 'I will focus on one task at a time' or 'I will speak kindly to myself today'. Intentions can be written in a journal or placed somewhere visible, like their phone wallpaper or mirror.

   Setting intentions helps teens and young adults approach their goals and challenges with clarity and purpose, fostering self-discipline and a positive mindset.

5. **Introduce the practice of 'noticing without judging'**
   Invite them to observe their thoughts and feelings without immediately judging them as 'good' or 'bad'. For example, if they feel frustrated, they might say, 'I'm noticing frustration,' rather than 'I shouldn't feel this way.'
   This practice builds self-compassion and reduces self-criticism, helping them accept their emotions and respond calmly. It cultivates a non-judgmental, resilient mindset that promotes emotional well-being.

Managing Mindfully: Bringing Awareness into the Workplace

Just as mindfulness can strengthen our relationships with family, it can also transform our relationships at work. If you are a manager for example, you have the opportunity to set the tone for a balanced, mindful work environment. A mindful manager leads with awareness, patience, and presence. This approach helps to create a team culture where everyone feels seen, heard, and valued. By bringing mindfulness into our management style, we can enhance our team's productivity, well-being, and sense of belonging.

Practicing mindful management benefits both managers and teams by reducing stress, building trust, and creating an environment where everyone feels appreciated and empowered. When we bring mindfulness into the workplace, we're not just managing tasks and crossing out deliverables; we're building a resilient, balanced, and harmonious team that thrives together and are highly engaged.

1. **Creating space for open communication**
   Mindful management starts with active listening and creating space for open communication. Instead of jumping to solutions or rushing through conversations,

a mindful manager takes a moment to fully listen and understand the needs and concerns of team members. This involves being present in conversations, setting aside distractions, and giving employees the time and attention they deserve.

For instance, if a team member is facing a challenge, a mindful manager listens actively, asks thoughtful questions, and shows genuine empathy. This approach not only strengthens trust but also helps employees feel seen and supported, creating a more positive and collaborative work environment.

2. **Responding rather than reacting**

   A mindful manager approaches situations with patience, aiming to respond rather than react. When faced with a stressful situation—whether it's a missed deadline, a miscommunication, or a challenging project—taking a mindful pause can help us respond with clarity and composure.

   By practicing this pause, we're less likely to let emotions drive our decisions, allowing us to choose responses that are balanced and constructive. This can involve taking a few deep breaths, briefly stepping away from a heated conversation, or taking time to reflect before giving feedback. Responding mindfully improves not only our decision-making but also our team's overall morale and motivation.

3. **Encouraging self-care and balance**

   A mindful manager recognizes the importance of well-being and balance, both for themselves and their team. Encouraging breaks, respecting boundaries, and fostering an environment where self-care is valued can significantly improve team performance and reduce burnout.

Simple actions, like encouraging regular breaks, celebrating team achievements, or providing flexibility, when possible, support employees in maintaining a healthy work-life balance. Modelling these practices ourselves as managers shows our team that we prioritize well-being, which in turn encourages them to take care of themselves.

4. **Modelling emotional intelligence and empathy**

Mindfulness helps managers cultivate empathy and emotional intelligence, which are crucial for managing diverse teams with varied needs and personalities. By becoming more aware of our own emotions and responses, we're better able to understand and support the emotional needs of our team members.

For example, when team members face personal challenges, a mindful manager offers understanding and flexibility, allowing space for them to manage their needs without judgment. By modelling empathy, we create an inclusive and compassionate workplace where employees feel comfortable being authentic and bringing their best selves to work.

5. **Building a culture of presence and purpose**

Mindful management goes beyond individual interactions; it's about building a culture of presence and purpose within the team. By fostering awareness, encouraging reflection, and focusing on meaningful goals, we can inspire our team to stay connected to a sense of purpose in their work.

In practice, this might look like starting team meetings with a brief check-in, setting mindful goals that align with team values, or providing opportunities for team members to reflect on what they find meaningful in their roles. These small practices help create a sense of unity and purpose, keeping the team motivated and engaged.

Showing Up for Ourselves

As with any skill, the key to building mindfulness and meditation into our lives is regularity. It's not about meditating perfectly or staying mindful all day; it's about showing up for ourselves regularly. Even a few minutes a day can make a difference, helping us create a habit of staying present and calm.

In my own journey, I've learned that real growth happens in small moments—like choosing to pause and breathe instead of reacting. This is what is called 'the sacred pause', a pause that you take when an emotional trigger arises. It allows you to take a brief step outside of the situation, observe what emotions rise to the surface for you, and respond to them and the situation in a more reasonable, calm, and thoughtful manner. These little choices add up, helping us build a life that feels more even-tempered and centred.

By now, we've explored how mindfulness and meditation can transform our lives. My greatest hope is that this practice will one day become second nature to all of us, much like brushing our teeth in the morning before we face our day and at night just before we go to bed.

In the succeeding section, we will look at how we can deepen our meditation and mindfulness practices, and how we can use small, simple moments throughout the day to stay grounded and present.

1. **The power of consistency**
   One of the most important parts of any practice is showing up. It doesn't have to be a huge time commitment; even just a few minutes a day can make a big difference. What's most important is the intention we bring to each practice

and our commitment to stick with it, even on days when we might not feel like it.

Imagine that every time we meditate or practice mindfulness, we're adding a drop of calm, clarity, and presence into our lives. Over time, those drops add up, creating a steady foundation that helps us face life's ups and downs with more ease. Consistency is what transforms these practices from occasional stress relief into powerful tools for real change.

Research supports this idea. Studies on regular mindfulness practice show that it builds resilience over time. Barbara Fredrickson's research on the broaden-and-build theory shows that when we regularly experience positive emotions, we strengthen our ability to cope with stress. This means that by committing to mindfulness and meditation, we're building a mental foundation that helps us feel balanced, no matter what life throws at us.

In my experience, real growth happens in those small, daily moments. It's in the times when I catch myself feeling distracted or stressed and choose to take a mindful breath instead. These little decisions build up, helping me stay grounded and connected to my deeper intentions.

2. **Using everyday moments as mindfulness practice**
While meditation is often a more formal practice, mindfulness is something we can bring into our daily lives anytime, anywhere. By bringing a bit of awareness to ordinary moments, we turn them into opportunities to reconnect with ourselves and the present moment.

For instance, we might practice mindfulness while brushing our teeth, focusing on the feel of the brush, the taste of the toothpaste, and the movement of our hands. Or we might practice mindfulness while washing dishes, paying attention to the warmth of the water, the texture of the soap, and the gentle clinking of the dishes.

Even taking a mindful breath before starting a task or pausing to notice the sights and sounds around us can be a way to build mindfulness into our day. These small acts may seem simple, but they help us create a habit of awareness that brings us back to the present moment, even during busy or challenging times.

3. **Reflecting on the journey**
   As we continue to practice mindfulness and meditation, it's also helpful to take time to reflect on our progress. What changes have we noticed? What challenges have we faced? Reflection helps us appreciate how far we've come and can motivate us to keep going, even on days when the practice feels difficult.

   One way to do this is by keeping a simple journal. Each day, we can write down a few sentences about how we feel after meditation, any insights that came up, or any small shifts we noticed in our mood or energy. This journal becomes a record of our journey, showing us how our practice is slowly transforming our lives in ways we may not have noticed otherwise.

4. **Creating a lifelong practice**
   As we build mindfulness and meditation into our lives, it becomes clear that this journey isn't about reaching a finish line—it's about cultivating a way of being that we carry with us every day. There will be ups and downs, days when meditation feels easy and days when it feels like a struggle. There will even come a point when your meditation becomes stale and boring, a sign that you are ready for the next level in deepening the practice. Each time we return to the practice, we strengthen our

foundation, becoming more grounded, resilient, and open to life.

With time and commitment, mindfulness and meditation become more than just practices—they become part of who we are. They give us the inner strength to face life's challenges with calm and clarity, to experience deeper joy and peace, and to connect more fully with ourselves and others. And as we continue on this path, we may find that the practice doesn't just change us—it changes the world around us, bringing more peace, kindness, and understanding into our lives and the lives of those we touch.

Meditation Starter

Meditation is a powerful and positive ritual that helps us slow down, feel present, and reconnect with a source that's bigger than ourselves. By creating this new ritual, you're adding calm, clarity, and balance to your life. The following suggestions will guide you through simple daily practices to help you start building this meditation ritual, with a focus on bringing your brain and heart into coherence—a state of calm and balance where your body feels aligned and at ease. Let's get started!

1. **Setting up your space**
   Choose a spot where you can sit comfortably and won't be interrupted. This doesn't have to be anything fancy—just a place where you can relax and feel at ease. Think of this space as a part of your new positive ritual.

2. **Daily practice log**
   Use this daily log to note your practice times, feelings, and any reflections that come up during meditation. Start with just five minutes each day, gradually increasing the time as you feel more comfortable. You may use the following cues to log your experience:

Table 6.2: An example of a daily practice log for meditation

Day	Time Spent Meditating	What I Focused On	How I Felt Before	How I Felt After
Day 1	e.g. 5 mins	e.g. Breath	e.g. Unsettled, tense shoulders	e.g. Reduced tension, feel more grounded

3. **Daily meditation guide**
   Each day, use the following steps to guide your meditation practice. Alternate between focusing on your breathing and practicing gratitude to bring your heart and brain into coherence. This positive ritual will help you feel more connected to yourself and the present moment.

   Breathing and heart awareness

   - **Get comfortable**: Sit quietly with your hands resting on your lap and close your eyes.
   - **Take three deep breaths**: Breathe in through your nose, filling your lungs, and breathe out slowly through your mouth.
   - **Focus on your heart**: Place your hand over your heart and bring your awareness to this area.
   - **Breathe into your heart**: Imagine that each breath flows in and out of your heart, creating a gentle rhythm.
   - **Notice how you feel**: Keep breathing slowly and focus on any sensations in your heart or chest area. Just stay present with it.

   Practicing gratitude for heart–brain coherence

   - **Get comfortable and breathe**: Settle in with a few deep breaths.
   - **Focus on your heart**: Bring your awareness to the centre of your chest, where your heart is.

- **Think of something you're grateful for**: This can be a person, a moment, or even something simple, like a warm cup of tea.
- **Feel the gratitude in your heart**: As you hold this thought, try to feel gratitude in your heart. Imagine it filling your chest with a warm green light that slowly radiates from the centre of your heart and forming an energetic field around you.
- **Stay with this feeling**: Keep focusing on the feeling of gratitude, breathing deeply and calmly. Let this feeling connect your heart and mind, creating a sense of peace.

4. **Reflection questions**

   At the end of each day, take a moment to reflect on this positive ritual. Answering these questions can help you notice patterns and make it easier to keep the habit going.
   - What did I enjoy about today's meditation?
   - What was challenging?
   - Did I notice any changes in my body or mood?
   - How did focusing on my heart make me feel?

5. **Weekly review**

   At the end of the week, review your practice. Reflect on what you enjoyed and any small changes you've noticed as you build this positive ritual into your life.
   - How did my mood or stress levels change over the week?
   - Do I feel more connected to myself or my surroundings?
   - Is there something I want to adjust next week?

6. **Tips for building your positive ritual of meditation**
   - **Set a reminder**: Choose a time each day that works for you and set a reminder to help you stay consistent.
   - **Start small**: Just five minutes is enough to start. You can increase your time as you feel comfortable.

- **Be patient**: It's normal for the mind to wander. Just gently bring your focus back to your heart or your breath.
- **Celebrate small wins**: Notice how you feel after each session. Celebrate the fact that you showed up for yourself, even if it was just for a few minutes.

Congratulations on starting this positive ritual!

With each practice, you're creating a ritual that helps bring your mind and heart into coherence. This state of balance and calm can bring more clarity, peace, and well-being into your life over time. Embrace this new ritual and the positive energy it brings!

Chapter 6 Summary: Practice Mindfulness and Meditation

In this chapter, we explored the nature of mindfulness and meditation, focusing on their transformative impact on mental, emotional, physical, and spiritual well-being. Drawing from personal experiences and scientific insights, the chapter demonstrates how these practices have evolved from mystical tools into practical, life-sustaining rituals. It emphasizes their role in fostering resilience, emotional balance, and healing, making them indispensable in navigating both daily challenges and profound life events. Mindfulness and meditation are presented as learnable skills that, when practiced consistently, can reshape not just our internal world but also the way we connect with others and experience life.

5 Key Takeaways

1. **Mindfulness and meditation as distinct but complementary practices**
   - Mindfulness is the art of being present in the moment without judgment, applicable to any daily activity—eating, walking, or conversing.

- Meditation is a more focused practice of stillness and introspection, creating dedicated space for deeper self-awareness.
- Together, they form a powerful duo, with mindfulness grounding us in the now and meditation enhancing our ability to respond with clarity and calm.

2. **The science of mindfulness and meditation**
   - Regular practice rewires the brain through neuroplasticity, enhancing focus, emotional regulation, memory, and resilience.
   - Key areas impacted include the prefrontal cortex (focus and control), amygdala (stress response), and hippocampus (emotional stability).
   - These changes are not just psychological but physiological, offering tangible benefits for overall health and well-being.

3. **The role of energy and heart–brain coherence**
   - Meditation helps balance the body's energy centres (chakras), creating harmony between emotional and physical health.
   - Practices like focusing on the heart centre foster heart–brain coherence, a state where emotional and cognitive rhythms align. This harmony boosts mental clarity, reduces stress, and supports the body's natural healing mechanisms.

4. **Practical applications for daily life**
   - Mindfulness and meditation can be seamlessly integrated into everyday routines. Practices like mindful breathing, mindful eating, or mindful listening cultivate presence and connection.
   - For parents, mindful parenting strengthens relationships and fosters emotional resilience in children, creating a more harmonious family environment.

- In the workplace, mindful management promotes a culture of awareness, trust, and balance, benefiting both leaders and teams.

5. **Consistency and reflection as keys to long-term growth**
    - The power of mindfulness and meditation lies in regular practice, even for a few minutes a day. Small, consistent actions build a foundation for resilience and clarity.
    - Reflecting on the journey—through journaling or self-assessment—helps track progress and deepen the practice over time.
    - The ultimate goal is not perfection but integration, making mindfulness and meditation second nature, much like brushing your teeth—a daily ritual that enhances overall well-being.

My Final Thoughts

Mindfulness and meditation are more than just techniques, they are life skills that enrich every facet of our existence. By cultivating these practices, we create space for growth, healing, and connection. This chapter invites readers to embark on this transformative journey, discovering how small, consistent steps can lead to profound, lasting change in both our inner and outer worlds.

CHAPTER 7

Practice Drawing Healthy Boundaries

> *'The only people who get upset about you setting boundaries are the ones who were benefiting from you having none.'*
>
> —Unknown

Freedom Lives Where Boundaries Begin

There is a paradoxical relationship between freedom and boundaries. True freedom isn't the absence of limits but the presence of well-defined personal boundaries that allow us to live authentically and without unnecessary stress, intrusion, or drama.

Healthy boundaries are the blueprint for authentic relationships and personal well-being. They are more than just rules we set for others. They are clear and empowering guidelines for how we engage in any type of relationship in order to protect our physical, emotional, and mental well-being. Think of them as a personal instruction manual that communicates to others how much time, energy, and resources we invest in different areas of our life. This helps us maintain a balance between responsibility and self-care.

Whether it's with loved ones or people we don't know well, boundaries act as the foundation that allows our relationships to really flourish. They are dictated by our own personal values and beliefs which act as our inner compass that give us the clarity and confidence needed to make sound decisions, especially when life throws us curve balls like competing priorities and high expectations. It is because of this that they are considered a necessity, not a luxury.

Some might view boundaries as barriers that inhibit true connection all together, but nothing can be further from the truth. The confusion often comes from failing to differentiate boundaries from self-sabotage. Self-sabotaging behaviours are like concrete walls that isolate us from others and block personal growth. Boundaries on the other hand, are like filters, they are permeable and flexible, designed to help us maintain balance and authenticity. Healthy boundaries do not hinder relationships, they strengthen them. When expressed in a healthy way, they create mutual respect, help to manage expectations, and most of all it empowers individuation.

Here are some of the ways setting boundaries can set us free:

1. **Freedom to define our space**

   Boundaries create a framework for how we interact with the world and how others interact with us. They establish our emotional, physical, and mental limits. When we know and respect these limits, we feel safe, secure, and in control of our lives, which is the foundation of true freedom.

2. **Freedom from overwhelm**

   Without boundaries, we may find ourselves overcommitted, emotionally drained, or burdened by the expectations of others. Setting boundaries protects our time, energy, and mental well-being, giving us the freedom to focus on what truly matters.

3. **Freedom to be ourselves**

   Boundaries allow us to live authentically, making decisions based on our values and needs rather than external pressures or guilt. They give us the freedom to say 'no' to things that don't serve us, enabling us to say 'yes' to what aligns with our goals and well-being.

4. **Freedom in relationships**
   Healthy boundaries foster mutual respect and understanding in our relationships. They prevent resentment, misunderstandings, and over-dependence, creating space for our relationships to thrive. With clear boundaries, we can connect with others while still maintaining our sense of self.

5. **Freedom through responsibility**
   By setting boundaries, we take responsibility for our lives. This empowerment creates a sense of freedom because we're no longer at the mercy of others' demands or expectations. By knowing where our boundaries begin, we carve out the space to live freely, authentically, and with purpose.

Values and Beliefs Are the Heart of Decision-Making

Decision-making is probably the hardest part to execute when it comes to boundary-setting. Boundaries set without a clear understanding of your values and beliefs are shaky at best. Our values and beliefs are what I call our *non-negotiables*. This is the one thing that can save us from vacillating when it comes to making the hard choice between saying yes and saying no. Without these, we become susceptible to outside influence, leaving us vulnerable to guilt, manipulation, and self-doubt. These are the lines we draw for ourselves that we're unwilling to cross, no matter what. They come from a deep understanding of who we are and what is important to us. These non-negotiables serve as our north star for when we find ourselves pulled in different directions due to high expectations, conflicting priorities, or pressure from others. In essence, they help us navigate the oftentimes confusing roadmap of life.

The process of setting boundaries becomes easier when you are clear with your values and beliefs. Without that as our foundation, boundary-setting can feel like nothing but a personal whim, aimless, or even confusing. When we don't know what we truly stand for, it becomes all too easy to say 'yes' to things that don't serve us, or 'no' to opportunities that could have been beneficial for us. As the famous saying goes, 'If you don't stand for something, you'll fall for anything.' Our values are what help us draw the line between what is acceptable and what isn't, both in terms of how we are treated by others and how we treat ourselves. It can significantly reduce the stress of decision-making because you'll always have that north star to guide you. This helps in avoiding burnout, emotional exhaustion, and allows you to maintain a sense of inner peace.

If you're like most people, you're probably wondering, 'What's the difference between a value and a belief?' Fair ask, I get that question a lot in fact. Values and beliefs are closely related concepts, but they differ in significant ways. Here's how:

- **Values**
  Values are core principles that guide our actions and behaviours. They represent what is most important to us, such as honesty, generosity, freedom, or compassion. Values function as guiding principles that inform how we live our lives, make choices, and interact with others. They are about what we want to embody. The nature of values are more enduring and stable over time. While they can evolve, they tend to be consistent and deeply ingrained because they reflect our sense of identity. Values carry an emotional weight because they define what matters most to us. When we compromise our values, we tend to feel discomfort or dissonance with our true self.

  From a metaphor standpoint, think of values as *roots*. It conveys the idea of something deep, stable, and essential to growth, providing nourishment for everything else that we build in our lives. Just like roots, values can overlap and expand and there are dozens, if not hundreds, of values that people across many cultures can hold. Ultimately, the most important thing is identifying the values that are most meaningful to us, as they serve as the stronghold in our life, the thing that grounds us in who we truly are.

- **Beliefs**
  Beliefs on the other hand are convictions that we hold to be true, these are often based on our experiences, upbringing, culture, or knowledge. They shape how we interpret the world, ourselves, and others. Beliefs are assumptions or understandings about how the world works. They often stem from what we have been taught, experienced, or internalized over time. Beliefs influence our thoughts, perceptions, and attitudes and can be subject to change as we gain new experiences or information. They are often tied to specific circumstances, and new realizations can sometimes lead us to modify our beliefs. These ideas are often based on what we believe is true.

  From a metaphorical standpoint, we can think of beliefs as *taglines* that articulate our own personal brand to the world. They are concise and impactful phrases that capture truths that we hold dear to us. Beliefs reflect our identity, values, and worldview, helping others understand our essence and what we truly stand for.

Here are some examples of values and what a belief statement, that aligns with that value, might look like:

Table 7.1: Examples of alignment between values and beliefs statements

VALUE	BELIEF STATEMENT
Honesty	'Trust thrives where truth is told.' 'Clarity comes from transparency.' 'Truth is the foundation of lasting relationships.' 'Honesty is the currency of trust.'
Money	'Money is neutral; it's how we use it that defines its impact.' 'Wealth can be a force for good when guided by purpose and integrity.' 'Money amplifies intentions—it's the heart behind it that matters.' 'Financial abundance can empower positive change and support communities.'
Compassion	'Kindness heals and connects.' 'Compassion creates stronger communities.' 'Caring for others nourishes my soul.' 'A compassionate heart is a powerful force.'
Honour	'Honour is lived through actions, not words.' 'Principles guide us through adversity.' 'Living honourably is our truest legacy.' 'Honour is doing what's right, even when it is not convenient.'
Respect	'Treating others with respect is a basic human right.' 'Respect nurtures peace and collaboration.' 'Respect unlocks true connection.' 'We honour each other's uniqueness through respect.' 'Respect transforms relationships and communities.'

VALUE	BELIEF STATEMENT
Accountability	'You can delegate responsibility but never accountability.' 'Accountability is the path to trust.' 'True accountability strengthens your integrity.' 'When you own it, you grow from it.'
Growth	'Embrace failures as stepping stones.' 'Every experience is an opportunity to evolve.' 'Growth happens when we push past our comfort zone.' 'Every day offers a chance to grow.'
Freedom	'Living freely fuels creativity.' 'Freedom is to follow your own path.' 'Freedom empowers the soul to soar.' 'Freedom is the power to choose without fear of judgment.'
Creativity	'Innovation begins with a spark of creativity.' 'Creativity unlocks limitless possibilities.' 'Break the mould, create something new.' 'Creativity is the art of making the impossible possible.'
Community	'Stronger together, we rise.' 'United, we create lasting change.' 'We rise by lifting each other.' 'Community is the stronghold of nations.'
Balance	'Balance is the key to peaceful living.' 'Balance is the harmony of life.' 'In balance, we find clarity and peace.' 'Balance allows space for everything that matters.'

Boundaries Are a Form of Self Respect, Not Self-Sabotage

One of the biggest misconceptions people have about boundaries is that they are selfish and can sabotage relationships. In reality, they are a form of self-respect. They allow you to create a healthy environment where you can thrive and pursue your goals without unnecessary distractions or emotional baggage. When you set boundaries, you are communicating to the world that your well-being matters and that you are not willing to sacrifice it for short-term gains or external approval.

People sometimes feel guilt when setting boundaries because they worry it will hurt the other person's feelings or make them seem unavailable or even difficult. But the truth is, not setting boundaries leads to more dysfunction in, or the demise of, relationships in the long run. When boundaries are weak or non-existent, it often leads to negative emotions like resentment, frustration, and judgment. We may feel as though people are constantly taking advantage of us, but in reality, we're allowing it to happen by not clearly communicating our needs. Poor boundaries result in a lack of control over our own life. Instead of living in alignment with our values, we end up prioritizing the needs of others at the expense of our well-being.

This cycle of poor boundaries often leads to pent-up frustration, which can easily turn into resentment. We might start blaming others for how we feel, even though the problem stems from our inability to say no or set limits. While it's easy to point the finger at others for asking too much, the real issue lies in not having communicated our limits.

Judgment often follows when boundaries are unclear. When someone violates our unspoken boundary, it's easy to jump to conclusions about their intentions. We might start thinking they don't respect us, or that they're being selfish, when in fact, they may simply be unaware of our needs. Declaring clear boundaries eliminates the guessing game by letting people know exactly what's okay and what isn't, reducing the likelihood of misunderstandings.

How to Set and Communicate Boundaries

Setting boundaries is one thing but communicating them is just as important. After all, people can't respect boundaries they aren't aware of. The key to communicating boundaries effectively is clarity and consistency. When you set a boundary, be direct and unapologetic about your needs. There's no need to justify or apologize for your boundaries—simply state it as a fact.

Consistency is also crucial when it comes to boundary-setting. If you set a boundary but allow it to be crossed repeatedly, it loses its effectiveness. By consistently upholding your boundaries, you teach others to respect them, and over time, they will come to understand your limits without needing constant reminders.

It's important to remember that setting boundaries isn't about controlling others; it's about taking responsibility for your own well-being. You can't control how others will react to your boundaries, but you can control how you respond when they're crossed. By calmly reinforcing your boundaries, you maintain control over your personal space, your energy, and your time, rather than allowing others to dictate your limits.

Another effective way to communicate boundaries is to express them with empathy, especially in personal relationships. Instead of framing your boundaries as rigid demands, you can frame them in a way that shows you value the relationship. For example, in a personal relationship, you could say, 'I really value our time together, but I also need time to recharge. Can we find a balance that works for both of us?' This approach invites collaboration and helps the other person understand your needs without feeling alienated.

Fear and Guilt

Let's face it, the biggest hurdle we all face when making our boundaries known is fear and guilt. Too often, these stop us from drawing healthy boundaries because they tap into deep emotional and subconscious patterns. But, when we recognize that fear and guilt are common but unnecessary barriers, we can begin to assert ourselves in a way that honours our values and needs without sacrificing our well-being. Here's a closer look at why these emotions can get in the way big time:

- **Fear of losing relationships**: Many people fear that by setting boundaries, they will disappoint or alienate others. This fear of rejection or abandonment can lead to hesitation in asserting personal limits, especially in relationships where approval and acceptance are important.
- **Fear of conflict**: Setting boundaries can sometimes lead to confrontation, and many people fear conflict. This fear can stem from a desire to avoid uncomfortable or challenging conversations.
- **Fear of being seen as selfish**: Society often praises selflessness and giving, which can create fear that setting boundaries might be seen as selfish or inconsiderate, even when it's necessary for well-being.
- **Guilt of letting others down**: Many people feel a sense of responsibility for the happiness and well-being of others, especially loved ones. This can make it hard to set boundaries, as the person feels guilty for not being as available or giving as they think they should be.
- **Guilt over prioritizing self-care**: People can feel guilty for prioritizing their own needs, especially if they've been conditioned to believe that putting others first is the 'right' thing to do. This guilt can create a conflict between self-care and the urge to constantly give to others.
- **Guilt from cultural or familial expectations**: Cultural and family values sometimes encourage people to sacrifice their own needs for others, leading to guilt when attempting to set boundaries that honour personal space or autonomy.

- **Seeking validation**: If someone's self-worth is tied to pleasing others or being liked, they may avoid setting boundaries out of fear that doing so will result in criticism or disapproval.
- **Believing their needs don't matter**: Individuals who struggle with self-worth may believe their needs are less important than others'. This can lead to guilt or fear when trying to assert boundaries, as they feel unworthy of protecting their own space or time.
- **Cultural conditioning**: Many people grow up in environments where boundaries were either discouraged or never modelled. They may fear the consequences of setting boundaries because it goes against what they've been taught.
- **Social expectations**: There are often societal pressures, especially for women, to be nurturing and accommodating. This can create guilt when attempting to set boundaries, as it goes against traditional expectations.

How to Overcome Fear and Guilt When Setting Boundaries

- **Start small**: Begin by setting small boundaries in low-stakes situations. This can help you build confidence in expressing your needs without feeling overwhelmed by fear or guilt.

- **State your boundary clearly:** State your boundary in a clear, calm and respectful manner. Be specific about what you need. Example: 'I need to keep my evenings free after 6 p.m. for time with my family.'

- **Offer options or alternatives:** After stating your boundary, offer a solution that accommodates both your needs and theirs. This shows you are willing to collaborate and find a middle ground.

Examples:

- *Time-based alternatives:* 'I won't be available after 7 p.m., but I can help you tomorrow morning.'
- *Task-based alternatives*: 'I can't take on this extra project right now, but I'm happy to assist by sharing resources or pointing you to someone who might be able to help.'

- **Use 'yes' before 'no' when appropriate:** Frame your boundary in a positive way, offering what you can do before mentioning what you can't.
  Example: 'I'd love to help, but I can only commit to an hour today. Would that work for you?'

- **Empower them to choose:** Let the other person know they have options to choose from, which can ease potential tension or disappointment.
  Example: 'I won't be available for dinner this Friday, but I'm free on Saturday or Sunday. Which works best for you?'

- **Offer compromises if possible:** If the situation allows, find a middle ground that protects your boundary while still addressing the other person's needs.
  Example: 'I can't stay late every night this week, but I can work an extra hour on Thursday to help with the deadline.'

- **Maintain flexibility without sacrificing your boundary:** Ensure that any options or alternatives you offer do not compromise your boundary. Flexibility should respect both parties' needs.
  Example: 'I can't lend you money, but I'm happy to help you explore other options like setting up a budget or finding other resources.'

Healthy Boundaries and Success

Some people fear that setting boundaries will sabotage their success, particularly in competitive environments like the workplace. They worry that saying no to extra tasks or setting limits on their time will make them seem less dedicated or ambitious. However, the reality is that healthy boundaries are essential for long-term success because they help you maintain balance, focus, and mental clarity. Without boundaries, you risk overcommitting and spreading yourself too thin, which ultimately undermines your ability to perform at your best.

In fact, many successful people attribute their accomplishments to their ability to set boundaries. They know that saying yes to everything doesn't lead to success—it leads to burnout. By focusing on what truly matters and protecting their time and energy, they're able to achieve more while maintaining their well-being. Setting boundaries allows them to prioritize their most important tasks for the day as well as their long-term goals, ensuring that they don't waste energy on things that don't align with their long-term vision.

Setting boundaries also helps us avoid the trap of perfectionism. Many high achievers feel the need to be everything to everyone, which leads to unrealistic expectations and constant self-criticism. By setting boundaries around our expectations of ourselves, we can let go of the pressure to be perfect and focus on making consistent progress instead. This mindset shift is crucial for long-term success because it allows us to sustain our efforts without becoming depleted.

Whether it's success in our career, personal development, or relationships, boundaries help us stay focused and prevent distractions from pulling us off course. When we have clear boundaries, we can allocate our time and energy to the things that truly matter, allowing us to make steady progress toward our goals.

Dealing with Boundary Violations

Even with clear communication, there will be times when your boundaries are crossed. This is natural, especially if you're in the process of establishing new boundaries with people who are used to you being more flexible or accommodating. The key to handling boundary violations is to address them calmly and assertively. Don't wait for resentment to build up. If someone crosses a boundary, kindly but firmly remind them of it.

It's also important to recognize that boundary violations aren't always intentional. Sometimes people overstep because they don't realize how important your boundary is to you. By addressing the issue directly and with kindness, you give the other person an opportunity to adjust their behaviour without feeling attacked.

If someone repeatedly violates your boundaries, despite clear communication, it may be necessary to reassess the relationship. Persistent boundary violations can be a sign that the other person doesn't respect your needs, which can be toxic to your well-being. In such cases, you may need to distance yourself from the relationship or seek professional guidance, such as therapy or counselling, to navigate the situation.

The Role of Self-Awareness in Setting Boundaries

Setting effective boundaries requires a deep sense of self-awareness. We need to know what our limits are, what makes us feel overwhelmed, and what drains our energy. Without this understanding, it's difficult to set boundaries that truly protect our well-being. Self-awareness helps us identify areas in our life where boundaries are lacking, allowing us to take proactive steps to improve those areas.

Self-awareness also plays a key role in preventing over-commitment. Many people struggle with saying no because they fear hurting other people's feelings or being seen as uncaring. However, constantly saying yes to others often means constantly saying no to ourselves. By becoming more aware of our energy levels, emotional triggers, and personal priorities, we will be better equipped to set boundaries that align with our well-being.

For instance, if you notice that socializing drains you after a long day of work, you can set a boundary around how often you engage in social activities during the week. Or if you find that certain conversations leave you feeling emotionally drained, you can set boundaries around the types of discussions you engage in. The more in tune you are with your own needs, the easier it becomes to set boundaries that support your well-being.

Boundaries Lead to Emotional Freedom

The ultimate goal of setting boundaries is to create a life of emotional freedom. When we establish clear boundaries, we give ourselves the space to be our authentic self without the constant fear of being overburdened, taken advantage of, or emotionally drained. Boundaries allow us to live in alignment with our non-negotiables, which leads to greater self-confidence and a stronger sense of self.

In relationships, emotional freedom means being able to express our needs without fear of rejection or judgment. It's about cultivating mutual respect and understanding, where both parties feel valued and heard. This leads to healthier, more fulfilling relationships because both individuals are free to be themselves without compromising their needs.

Emotional freedom also comes from the knowledge that we have control over our own life. Instead of feeling trapped by external expectations, we can navigate life with clarity and intention. Boundaries free us from the need to please everyone and give us the courage to prioritize our own happiness and well-being.

Boundaries Make for Healthy Relationships for the Long Term

Boundaries are the foundation of healthy, respectful relationships. Without boundaries, relationships can quickly become unbalanced, with one person feeling overburdened or undervalued. Clear boundaries ensure that both individuals' needs are met, fostering mutual respect and understanding.

In romantic relationships, boundaries help maintain individuality while building a strong partnership. For example, each partner may need personal space or time apart to recharge, and setting boundaries around that need prevents feelings of suffocation or resentment. Similarly, boundaries around communication—such as agreeing not to discuss sensitive topics when emotions are running high—can prevent unnecessary conflicts and ensures that both partners feel heard and respected.

Friendships also benefit from clear boundaries. It's easy for friendships to become strained when one person consistently oversteps or when the expectations aren't clearly communicated. For instance, if a friend frequently asks for favours but doesn't reciprocate, resentment can build. Setting boundaries in friendships ensures that the relationship remains balanced and that both individuals feel valued.

In families, boundaries are essential for fostering respect and maintaining a healthy functioning dynamic. Family members often share close quarters and responsibilities, making it easy for personal boundaries to blur. By setting clear expectations around personal time, privacy, roles, and chores, family members can prevent misunderstandings and avoid conflict. For example, parents might need to set boundaries with their children around work or rest time, while siblings may need space for their own interests. Healthy boundaries in families allow for individual growth while strengthening the bonds of support and love, ensuring that everyone's needs are recognized and respected.

Boundaries Are the Key to a Balanced Life

All said and done, healthy boundaries are not about shutting people out or being rigid, they are about creating a balanced life where we can thrive emotionally, mentally, and physically. Boundaries set the guidelines for how we want to be treated and how we manage our time, energy, and emotions. They are rooted in our values and beliefs, helping us make decisions that protect our well-being without sabotaging our chances for success.

By setting and communicating clear boundaries, we create an environment where we can pursue our goals, nurture our relationships, and maintain our personal integrity. Boundaries empower us to take control of our lives, preventing feelings of resentment and burnout, and fostering emotional freedom and success. Ultimately, boundaries are not a form of self-sabotage—they are the key to a healthy, fulfilling, and balanced life.

Chapter 7 Summary: Practice Drawing Healthy Boundaries

In this chapter, we explored how healthy boundaries are essential for creating a life of balance, emotional freedom, and authentic relationships. They serve as a blueprint for how we interact with the world, manage our time and energy, and protect our mental and emotional well-being. Boundaries are not barriers; they are empowering guidelines that allow us to thrive while maintaining meaningful connections. Rooted in our values and beliefs, they provide clarity and confidence in decision-making, helping us navigate the complexities of life.

5 Key Takeaways

1. **Boundaries set us free**
   Boundaries are the foundation of true freedom. They help us define our space, protect our energy, and maintain control over our lives. Far from being restrictive, healthy boundaries empower us to live authentically and without unnecessary drama or being overwhelmed.

2. **Values and beliefs anchor our boundaries**
   Our values and beliefs act as a compass for setting and maintaining boundaries. They help us distinguish between what aligns with our priorities and what doesn't. By understanding our non-negotiables, we can make confident decisions, even in the face of external pressure or competing priorities.

3. **Communicating boundaries with clarity and empathy**
   Setting boundaries is only half the equation; clearly communicating them is equally important. Expressing our needs with calmness and respect makes for better understanding

and collaboration. Consistency in upholding boundaries with kindness teaches others to respect them, and this type of honesty strengthens our relationships over time.

4. **Overcoming fear and guilt to assert ourselves**
   Fear of conflict, rejection, or being seen as selfish can make boundary-setting difficult. Recognizing these emotions as natural but unnecessary barriers allows us to prioritize self-care without compromising our relationships. Starting small and practicing regularly builds confidence in asserting our needs.

5. **Boundaries strengthen relationships and creates balance**
   Healthy boundaries nurture trust, respect, and individuality in relationships. They prevent resentment, over-dependence, and misunderstandings, creating space for authentic connections to flourish. Whether in personal, familial, or professional relationships, clear boundaries promote harmony and mutual growth.

My Final Thoughts

Healthy boundaries help us prioritize where and how we invest our energy. By clearly outlining what we will and won't allow in our lives, we create space for what truly matters, reducing distractions and preventing emotional burnout. By practicing the art of setting and communicating boundaries, we create a balanced way of life, where our relationships thrive, our goals are protected, and our well-being is prioritized. Boundaries are not selfish; they are a profound act of self-respect and empowerment, enabling us to live with clarity, confidence, and freedom.

CHAPTER 8

The Power of Believing

> *'Whether you think you can, or you think you can't - you're right.'*
>
> –Henry Ford

If you've made it this far in the book, you might feel like you're almost there—that you now have everything you need to harness happiness and fulfilment in your life. But here's the truth: all of that is only half of the recipe. What makes it all work and come together, as it did for me, is what this final chapter is all about. I think of it as the secret sauce.

Sooner or later, we all meet our creations. Whether you choose to embrace every practice shared in the earlier chapters or focus on just one, your success ultimately boils down to a single, crucial factor—your belief. If you truly believe these practices will ignite change within you, they absolutely will. But if you don't, they certainly never will. Belief is the power that transforms effort into results, visions into realities.

Beliefs are the unseen architects of our reality, silently moulding our view of the world around us and how we see ourselves in it. It is a force that influences not only our sense of capability or limitation but, perhaps most importantly, it is the energy that fuels our sense of worth. If you believe you are worthy and deserving of a happy and fulfilling life, you will naturally create that reality for yourself. On the other hand, if you believe that others are out to get you or waiting for you to fail, you'll unconsciously attract situations that reinforce those fears.

However, when you choose to love life and believe that it is kind and generous, it has a way of returning that positivity and loving you back tenfold. Whether we realize it or not, our beliefs act as a lens, colouring how we interpret every experience. A positive belief system can inspire confidence, strengthen resilience, and support personal growth. In contrast, limiting beliefs quietly build walls that block success and jeopardize our well-being. Understanding this power allows us to consciously shape beliefs that align with our highest potential and uphold the life we want to create.

At their core, beliefs are unique to the individual. They are both deeply personal and profoundly impactful, but they are not always factual. They are interpretations, often formed through past experiences, cultural influences, and our own personal narratives. Our beliefs are our earliest inheritance from our parents and caregivers when we first came to this world—that much is fact. The rest is circumstantial. We are all victims of our upbringing, be it good or bad. Most of what we believe to be true about who we are was passed down to us by our parents, caregivers, and teachers during the first six years of our lives when we were like sponges, as they say. And sponges don't filter, they just absorb. A child who constantly hears phrases like 'You're bad' or 'Why can't you be more like . . . ?' may internalize the belief that they are inadequate and inferior to others even when their achievements later in life prove otherwise. Similarly, consistent encouragement and reinforcement of positive qualities such as creativity, determination, or kindness can nurture self-confidence and empower a child to believe in themselves and their value as a person.

Needless to say, all kinds of information that we absorbed became our so-called programmes , they were imprinted in our subconscious and worked quietly in the background like an operating system in a computer. We then carry these programmes throughout our lives unaware of our malware, until some type of breakdown forces us to look more deeply into who we are, how we are wired, and why we are the way we are. And just like any computer, we come to realize at some point in our lives that we could use a bit of a system upgrade, maybe even rewrite the code all together to build new systems that can turbo charge our well-being and our life.

The Neuroscience of Belief

Neuroscience reveals that beliefs are not abstract ideas but tangible patterns in the brain. They shape neural pathways, influencing how we process information and respond to stimuli. For instance, studies on neuroplasticity—the brain's ability to reorganize itself—show that repeated thought patterns, including beliefs, strengthen specific neural connections. This means that reinforcing positive beliefs through affirmations, visualization, or practice can literally rewire the brain to support a more optimistic and proactive mindset.

Conversely, negative beliefs can become deeply entrenched, creating cognitive biases that filter out evidence to the contrary. Someone who believes they are unworthy may disregard compliments or achievements, focusing instead on perceived flaws or failures. Over time, these biases reinforce the belief, making it harder to break the cycle.

Beliefs Are Self-Fulfilling Prophecies

Prophecies are predictive in nature; they describe events that are yet to happen often with a sense of certainty or inevitability. The term is commonly associated with spiritual, religious, or mystical contexts, but it can also be used metaphorically in many ways. A self-fulfilling prophecy in psychology is a concept where a belief or an expectation, whether about oneself or others, influences actions and behaviours in ways that cause the expectation to eventually come true. This concept emphasizes the powerful correlation between how we view things, the actions we take and the outcomes we create as a result.

Here is how self-fulfilling prophecies work. The process begins with a strong conviction or an expectation. For instance, one might believe that they will succeed at being an entrepreneur, or conversely, that they are no good in business and they are bound to fail. This belief will inevitably lead to attitudes, behaviours, and decisions congruent with that belief. Positive expectations can motivate one to take initiative and persist despite difficulties, while negative ones might cause hesitation or avoidance all together resulting in an outcome that reflects the belief. The action, or inaction, is what will lead to results that confirm the original belief, therefore fulfilling and perpetuating the cycle over and over.

This pattern has everything to do with how our brain's neural pathways work. Remember the saying, 'neurons that fire together, wire together'? The longer we hold onto a belief system, the stronger and more entrenched it becomes in our brain, convincing us it's true. The brain craves certainty because certainty feels safe. Familiarity is its comfort zone, and safety is its top priority. It doesn't care if we're successful, it only cares that we survive and stay alive.

That's why the brain will do everything it can to keep you from stepping outside your comfort zone. It will tell you not to bother preparing for something new, convince you to avoid risks at all costs, or to ignore creative ideas for innovation. Why? Because as far as it's concerned, you've made it this far without all that effort and risk-taking, so why rock the boat? Your brain doesn't know the difference between the threat of a saber-tooth tiger and the fear of failing at something new that might potentially levae you without a roof over your head . To your brain, fear is fear and keeping you safe and alive means it has done its job.

For some of us, the thought of achieving success might in fact feel intimidating and overwhelming. This seems counterintuitive but it's true. Some of us want success but deep down we don't really know what to do with it if we actually manage to get it. The responsibilities, the long hours, or even the recognition that comes with achieving something big can trigger self-doubt and we start to question whether we have what it takes to keep it up ('I'm not good enough'), or if we even deserve it ('I'm not worthy'). These questions push us back into our safe little corner, where we convince ourselves that we're not cut out for the challenges of entrepreneurship or any big dream for that matter. And just like that, we prove our own limiting beliefs before we even get the chance to try the alternative on for size.

Staying safe and staying stuck are two sides of the same coin. The reality is that this type of repeating pattern is our brain's way of trying to protect us, not a reflection of our actual abilities. To break free, we need to challenge those beliefs, push past the discomfort, and retrain our minds to embrace growth. Only then can we step out of the shadows and claim our place in the sun.

Breaking Negative Self-Fulfilling Prophecies

Negative self-fulfilling prophecies can quietly sabotage our dreams, often before they even take root. These self-imposed limitations stem from our deeply held beliefs about what we're capable of achieving. The good news? They're not permanent! By identifying, challenging, and reshaping these beliefs, we can step out of the shadows of self-doubt and into a space where visions have room to flourish.

Here's a deeper dive into the process of breaking free from negative self-fulfilling prophecies:

1. **Identify the belief**
   The first step is to recognize the limiting beliefs or expectations influencing our actions or inactions.

Many of us carry subconscious narratives formed from past experiences, societal influence, or fear of failure. These beliefs may manifest as thoughts like:

- 'I'm not cut out to be a leader.'
- 'I'm not smart enough to run my own business.'
- 'If I fail, everyone will judge me.'

Example: One of my clients, an aspiring entrepreneur, wants to start a graphic design agency. Every time she thinks about pitching her services, a voice in her head tells her, 'You're not as talented as other designers.' This belief prevents her from taking steps like reaching out to potential clients or showcasing her work on social media. As a result, her business stagnates before it even begins, reinforcing her initial belief that she's not good enough to put herself out in the market.

Action step: To bring this deep-seated belief to the surface I asked her to reflect on the following questions:

- 'What are you afraid of?'
- 'Where does this belief come from?'
- 'Does this belief help or hinder you?'

Awareness is the first step toward breaking free from the cycle. Go ahead and ask yourself the same questions and see what you might uncover.

2. **Challenge the belief**

   Once identified, the next step is to question the validity of the belief. Often, negative beliefs are based on assumptions rather than evidence. By challenging these beliefs, you can begin to see them for what they are—stories, not facts (see Chapter 4).

Reframe the belief by asking yourself:

- 'What evidence do I have that supports this belief?'
- 'Is this belief based on past experiences that no longer apply?'
- 'What advice would I give a friend who had this belief?'

Example: In the case of my client, her belief about not being talented enough stemmed from a harsh critique she received in college. But she also recognizes that since then, she has gained years of experience, received compliments from peers, climbed up the corporate ladder, and even had one of her projects featured on social media by a client who really loved her work. By focusing on these facts, she starts to reframe her belief:

- Original belief: 'I'm not talented enough to succeed.'
- Reframed belief: 'My skills have grown tremendously, and I am capable of delivering value to clients.'

Action step: In the same format as above, write down the limiting belief, or beliefs, you have identified and actively rewrite it into a positive, empowering statement. You could use this statement as a daily affirmation to help internalize the new perspective. Combine this new positive narrative with visualization and elevated emotions to establish new neural connections that will strengthen over time (see Chapter 6).

3. **Change behaviours**

Challenging a belief is essential, but it's the actions that follow that truly reshape our personal reality. To break a self-fulfilling prophecy, you need to take steps that align with the new, empowering belief. Fair warning though, this change will feel very uncomfortable at first. If it's not giving off uncomfortable vibes then you're doing it all wrong, it means you're still doing the familiar and you're not really doing enough to make any significant change.

Small, consistent actions are key. Start by taking manageable steps toward your goal. Each action you take builds evidence that supports your new belief, weakening the hold of the old one.

Example: For my client, the first small step she decided to take was creating a portfolio of her best work and sharing it online. Having this digital material available gave her a sense of legitimacy in the market and gave her the confidence to reach out to one potential client per week or attend a networking event to connect with other designers for possible collaboration. These actions may initially feel daunting, but by holding herself accountable and showing up to these commitments—one day at a time—reinforces a new positive belief in her ever-evolving talents and capabilities.

Action step: Be intentional in generating your momentum. Small actions create momentum, and momentum is what builds self-confidence. Over time, these micro wins add up, making it easier to take on bigger challenges (see Chapter 5).

4. **Reinforce New Patterns**

Breaking a self-fulfilling prophecy isn't a one-time effort, it's an ongoing process. Reinforcing new, positive patterns helps solidify the belief and create lasting change. Celebrating progress, no matter how small, plays a crucial role in this reinforcement.

Celebrate successes. Every win, whether it's landing a new client, completing a project, or simply stepping out of your comfort zone to show up at a networking event, deserves recognition. Celebrating these achievements rewires your brain to associate effort with success, further reinforcing the new positive belief.

Example: After securing a new project, my client took the time to acknowledge her progress. She reflects on how her actions—sharing her portfolio, pitching her services, and challenging her fears—led to landing a contract. This reflection strengthens her belief that she is capable and deserving of success. She also leveraged on positive feedback from others to reinforce new patterns. Whenever she encounters negative feedback, she reframes this as encouragement to update her skills to stay relevant and in touch with her customer's needs.

Action step: Incorporate habits that align with your new belief. For example, if you're building confidence as an entrepreneur, set a weekly goal to pitch your business to at least one person or take a skill-enhancing course. Over time, these routines become second nature, reinforcing the belief that you're proactive, capable, and committed (see Chapter 5).

Overcoming Common Challenges

Breaking negative self-fulfilling prophecies isn't always easy. It requires conscious awareness and intentionality. Here are some common challenges we might face and strategies to overcome them:

1. **Fear of failure**
   Fear can paralyse action, making it hard to take the first step. It helps to remind ourselves that failure is a natural part of growth and an opportunity to learn. Instead of

viewing failure as a reflection of your worth, see it as a stepping stone to success.

   - Reframe: When you are nervous about putting anything out there, focus on service. When we place ourselves in the position of being in the service of something, the pressure to perform falls away and selflessness takes over.

2. **Imposter syndrome**
   Many entrepreneurs struggle with feeling like they don't deserve their success. Counter this by focusing on your achievements and the value you bring to others.
   - Action step: Keep a 'success journal' where you document accomplishments, positive feedback, and milestones. File them away where you can easily find them for days when your confidence needs a good boosting.

3. **Resistance to change**
   Breaking old patterns takes effort, and your brain's first instinct is to resist. Stay committed to your new behaviours, especially if they feel uncomfortable, that's how you know you are changing.
   - Mindset shift: Recognize discomfort as a sign of growth. The most effective changes are the ones that make you feel most uncomfortable. If the feeling is predictable, then you are likely still in your comfort zone.

The Ripple Effect of Breaking Negative Beliefs

As you challenge and replace negative beliefs, the changes in your mindset and actions can have a ripple effect on your life's journey:

- **Enhanced confidence**: You'll approach opportunities with a mindset of possibility rather than fear.

- **Stronger relationships**: Beliefs about trust and collaboration can improve interactions with clients, partners, and employees.
- **Increased creativity**: Letting go of limiting beliefs frees your mind to explore innovative ideas.
    - *Example*: My client's journey didn't stop at securing her first client. With her newfound confidence, she begins offering free workshops to teach others about graphic design, expanding her business beyond what she initially thought possible. Each step reinforces her belief in her abilities, creating a positive feedback loop and new neural connections that reinforced her newfound confidence in herself.

Never forget, negative self-fulfilling prophecies are not permanent. By identifying limiting beliefs, challenging their validity, taking aligned actions, and reinforcing new patterns, we can break free from the constraints of self-doubt. The journey requires persistence and courage, but the rewards of personal growth, professional success, and fulfilment are worth the effort. Remember, the key to rewriting your story is believing in the possibility of a better one and taking the steps to make it real. As you challenge old beliefs and replace them with empowering ones, you'll discover that success is not just achievable—it's inevitable.

The Law of Belief

I want to support this perspective on beliefs further by talking about The Law of Belief. It is a principle that underscores the profound influence our beliefs have on our lives, shaping how we perceive the world, make decisions, and ultimately experience reality. Rooted in metaphysical teachings, personal development philosophies, and psychological principles, the Law of Belief suggests that what you believe to be true becomes true for you. While this concept may not be a formal scientific law, its impact is evident in countless areas of life, from personal growth and relationships to health and success.

At its core, the Law of Belief is simple: Your beliefs act as lenses through which you interpret the world. These lenses influence your thoughts, emotions, actions, and even the outcomes you achieve. Whether positive or negative, empowering or limiting, beliefs create a framework for how you navigate life.

This principle aligns with the idea of self-fulfilling prophecies, where beliefs shape behaviour in ways that make those beliefs manifest. For example, someone who believes they are capable of achieving their goals is likely to take proactive steps toward success, while someone who doubts their abilities may hesitate, leading to stagnation.

Psychological Foundations of the Law of Belief

The Law of Belief is supported by principles in psychology, particularly cognitive behavioural theory (CBT). According to CBT, our thoughts (shaped by beliefs) directly influence our emotions and behaviours. For instance, if you believe 'I am not good enough', this belief can lead to feelings of inadequacy and actions that reinforce failure, such as avoiding challenges or opportunities. Conversely, the belief 'I am capable of learning and improving' fosters confidence, persistence, and success.

Another psychological concept relevant to the Law of Belief is confirmation bias. This cognitive bias causes people to seek out evidence that supports their existing beliefs while ignoring or dismissing contradictory information. For example, someone who believes they are unlucky may focus on minor setbacks while overlooking positive outcomes, reinforcing the perception that luck is always against them.

How the Law of Belief Shapes Reality

1. **Beliefs influence perception**
   Beliefs determine how we interpret events and experiences. Two people facing the same situation may perceive it entirely differently based on their belief systems. For instance, a person who believes that challenges are opportunities for growth will view setbacks as temporary and surmountable. On the other hand, someone who believes they are doomed to fail may see the same setback as proof of their limitations.

2. **Beliefs drive behaviour**
   What you believe about yourself and the world influences your actions. A belief in one's ability to succeed motivates action, while self-doubt often leads to procrastination or avoidance. Over time, these behaviours create patterns that reinforce the original belief.

3. **Beliefs shape relationships**
   Beliefs about others—whether they are trustworthy, kind, or untrustworthy—affect how we interact with them. A belief in open communication fosters connection, while mistrust can create distance and conflict. These dynamics can shape the quality of relationships and, by extension, one's overall well-being.

4. **Beliefs directly impact health**
   The placebo effect is a striking example of how beliefs influence physical reality. When patients believe a treatment will work, their bodies often respond positively, even if the treatment is inactive. This phenomenon highlights the power of belief to affect not only mental states but also biological processes.

5. **Beliefs create opportunities or limitations**
   The Law of Belief suggests that opportunities arise when you believe in their possibility. For instance, believing 'there is always a way forward' inspires creative problem-solving and persistence, while a belief in scarcity or failure closes off avenues for exploration.

Examples of the Law of Belief in Action

1. **Personal development**
   Imagine a person trying to learn a new skill. If they believe 'I'm too old to learn new things,' they are unlikely to invest the necessary time and effort, and this belief becomes a self-fulfilling prophecy. In contrast, someone who believes 'it's never too late to grow' approaches the challenge with curiosity and persistence, leading to eventual mastery.

2. **Professional success**
   An entrepreneur who believes in their vision is more likely to persevere through obstacles, attract collaborators, and take calculated risks. Their belief acts as a driving force behind their success. Conversely, doubt can paralyse action, stalling progress.

3. **Health and healing**
   The placebo effect demonstrates how belief in the efficacy of a treatment can lead to actual improvements in health. Similarly, individuals with a strong belief in their body's ability to heal often experience faster recovery and better outcomes than those who hold pessimistic views.

4. **Social dynamics**
   Beliefs about social roles and norms shape how people behave in group settings. For example, a belief in teamwork and shared

goals fosters collaboration, while a belief in competition and scarcity can lead to conflict and division.

Beliefs are Malleable

The most empowering aspect of the Law of Belief is that beliefs are malleable. While deeply ingrained beliefs may feel permanent, they can be challenged and reshaped. Here's how:

1. **Self-awareness**
   The first step is to identify your core beliefs. Journaling, mindfulness, and introspection can help uncover unconscious beliefs driving your thoughts and actions. Ask questions like, 'What do I believe about myself? About success? About others?'

2. **Challenging limiting beliefs**
   Once identified, limiting beliefs can be challenged by examining their validity. For instance, if you believe, 'I'm not good at public speaking,' reflect on past experiences. Were there moments of success you've overlooked? Reframe the belief as, 'I'm improving my public speaking skills through practice.'

3. **Reinforcing empowering beliefs**
   Use affirmations, visualization, and positive self-talk to reinforce new beliefs. For example, repeat 'I am capable of achieving my goals' daily and visualize yourself succeeding in specific scenarios.

4. **Surrounding yourself with positive influences**
   Beliefs are influenced by the environments and people we engage with. Surround yourself with individuals who encourage growth and challenge limiting perspectives.

5. **Action and evidence**
   Take small, consistent actions to build evidence for your new beliefs. For instance, if you believe you can improve a skill, practicing regularly will reinforce this belief.

Balancing the Law of Belief

While the Law of Belief is empowering, it's important to balance it with realism. Beliefs alone cannot override external factors such as systemic barriers, resource limitations, or unforeseen challenges. Effort, strategy, and adaptability are necessary complements to belief. Additionally, overly rigid or unrealistic beliefs can lead to disappointment or harm if not tempered with critical thinking.

Integrating the Law of Belief into Daily Life

To harness the Law of Belief effectively:

- **Start small**: Focus on one belief you want to change and work consistently to reframe it.
- **Practice gratitude**: Cultivate a belief in abundance by regularly acknowledging what is going well in your life.
- **Stay mindful**: Monitor thoughts and beliefs that arise in challenging situations and consciously choose empowering interpretations.

The Law of Belief emphasizes the profound role of mindset in shaping our experiences and outcomes. By understanding and consciously shaping our beliefs, we gain the power to transform our lives. While effort, strategy, and action are essential, beliefs act as the foundation for all meaningful change. Whether in personal growth, relationships, health, or success, the Law of Belief reminds us that our inner world creates our outer reality. Just remember, the first step to achieving anything is believing that you can.

Chapter 8 Summary: The Power of Believing

This chapter reveals the vital role of belief in making meaningful changes in life. It emphasizes that belief is the secret ingredient that transforms the practices in this book into actionable, life-changing tools. Without belief, the most powerful strategies fall flat.

5 Key Takeaways

1. **Belief is the key to unlocking change**
   - The practices shared in this book can only work if you believe in their power to ignite change. Belief transforms effort into results and visions into reality. If you approach these practices with doubt or scepticism, you will unconsciously block their impact. On the other hand, a mindset rooted in belief allows these practices to work to their fullest potential.
     - *Example*: An entrepreneur trying a new strategy for networking must believe in its potential. Without belief, their hesitancy or lack of effort may lead to failure, reinforcing doubts about the strategy's value.

2. **Beliefs shape reality**
   - Beliefs are the unseen architects of life, colouring how we view ourselves and the world. They guide actions, influence decisions, and shape outcomes. Positive beliefs inspire confidence and resilience, while limiting beliefs block progress and diminish well-being. Whether you believe you can succeed or fail, your actions align with that belief, creating a self-fulfilling prophecy.
     - *Example*: A reader of this book who believes in their ability to implement the practices shared will approach each exercise with enthusiasm and consistency,

resulting in tangible improvements. A reader who doubts their capacity to change may give up too early, reinforcing the belief that change isn't possible.

3. **Beliefs begin early and operate subconsciously**
   - Most of our beliefs are shaped in childhood, absorbing messages from caregivers and experiences when we lacked the ability to filter them critically. These early 'programmes ' run in the background like software, influencing how we interpret events and respond to challenges. This book challenges readers to examine and rewrite these beliefs to create new patterns that empower growth.
     - *Example*: Someone raised with a belief like 'I'm not a leader' may hesitate to take charge in business ventures, even when they have the skills. Recognizing this belief as outdated and reframing it to 'I have the potential to grow into a great leader' opens doors to possibilities.

4. **Neuroscience shows belief is a powerful force**
   - Beliefs are not abstract ideas; they are neural patterns in the brain that shape how we process information. The concept 'neurons that fire together, wire together' explains how repeated thoughts strengthen neural pathways, making beliefs feel like undeniable truths. Positive beliefs can rewire the brain, while negative ones deepen cognitive biases that block growth.
     - *Key insight*: Reinforcing empowering beliefs through affirmations, visualization, and consistent practice rewires the brain to support a more optimistic and proactive mindset. To make the practices in this book effective, start by believing they can work.

5. **Breaking limiting beliefs is a process of action and reinforcement**
    - Limiting beliefs can quietly sabotage progress, but they are not permanent. This chapter outlines four steps to breaking free:
        - **Identify the belief:** Recognize the subconscious narratives that are holding you back.
        - **Challenge the belief**: Ask if it is based on evidence or assumptions and reframe it positively.
        - **Change behaviours**: Take small, deliberate actions that align with the new belief.
        - **Reinforce the new pattern**: Celebrate every success, no matter how small, to build confidence and solidify the change.
        - *Example*: A reader struggling with the belief 'I'm not good enough' might start by identifying moments of self-doubt, reframing them as 'I am constantly growing and improving,' and taking one small step toward a goal, like networking with potential collaborators. Over time, these actions reinforce their new belief.

My Final Thoughts

Belief is the foundation upon which all change is built. It is the root of transformation, the force that fuels our efforts and gives life to our dreams. The practices in this book are designed to guide you toward a life of happiness, fulfilment, and growth, but they are only as powerful as the belief you invest in them. Without belief, even the most effective tools remain dormant, their potential untapped. With belief, these practices become catalysts for extraordinary transformation.

Conclusion

Belief is not simply about optimism or wishful thinking, it is about choosing to trust in your own capacity to grow and evolve. It is about taking ownership of your narrative and deciding that you are worthy of the life you desire. If you believe these practices will work, they will. If you don't, they won't. It's that simple. This is because belief carries the energy and intention we bring to every action, infusing our efforts with the power to create real and lasting change.

The Courage to Believe

Belief requires courage. It asks you to embrace uncertainty and step into the unknown, trusting that the process will lead you somewhere meaningful. It demands that you silence the voice of self-doubt and choose a narrative of possibility instead. For many, this can feel uncomfortable or even impossible at first. After all, the comfort zone is where familiarity lives, and belief often requires breaking free from the stories you've told yourself for years—stories about your limitations, your worth, and what's possible for you.

But here's the truth: belief is also a skill. It can be nurtured, practiced, and strengthened over time. Like a muscle, it grows with use. By choosing to believe—one small step, one courageous action at a time—you train your mind to see opportunities instead of obstacles, to focus on solutions rather than setbacks.

Belief in Action

Throughout this book, I've shared practices that have the power to enhance your well-being and transform your life. Each of these practices is a seed, waiting to be planted and nurtured in the soil of your belief. Consider this:

- Self-awareness helps you identify the beliefs that shape your reality.
- Positive self-narratives allow you to rewrite the stories that no longer serve you.
- Positive rituals anchor your days in intention and purpose.
- Mindfulness and meditation cultivate the clarity to align your beliefs with your actions.
- Healthy boundaries protect the life you are building, ensuring it grows in alignment with your values.

These practices are your toolkit, but belief is the hand that wields them. Without belief, the tools lie unused. With belief, they become the most effective machinery for a life lived fully and intentionally.

The Cost of Doubt

Doubt can be seductive. It whispers that it's safer not to try, that you'll only fail, or that change is too difficult. It's a defence mechanism, your brain's way of keeping you safe from perceived risks. But the cost of doubt is high. It keeps you small, confined to the familiar, and stuck in a cycle of unmet potential.

When you choose not to believe, you unconsciously affirm the very limitations you wish to overcome. You reinforce the narrative that change isn't possible, that your dreams are out of reach, or that happiness is meant for someone else. This cycle only perpetuates itself, leaving you in the same place, year after year.

The Ripple Effect of Belief

When you choose belief, you create ripples that extend far beyond yourself. Belief fuels action, and action creates momentum. Over time, small steps compound into significant progress. The confidence you build in one area of life spills over into others. Your relationships improve as you approach them with greater clarity and authenticity. Your career flourishes as you embrace challenges with a growth mindset. Your health improves as you align your habits with a belief in your own vitality.

Belief doesn't just change your life—it inspires those around you. When others see the transformation belief has brought into your life, they may be inspired to question their own limiting beliefs and step into their potential. In this way, belief becomes a gift you give to the world, creating a legacy of possibility.

Your Journey Forward

As you close this book, I encourage you to carry one thought with you: belief is a choice. It is not always easy, but it is always available to you. Choose to believe in your ability to change and grow, even when it feels difficult. Choose to believe in the practices you've learned here, even if the results take time. Choose to believe in your worth, even if you're still learning to see it.

Well-being, happiness, and fulfilment are not destinations, they are ways of being that we practice throughout our lives. They are the result of showing up each day with intention, effort, and strong conviction. The journey won't always be smooth, but it will always be worth it. You have everything you need to create the life you want and the person you aspire to be. Everything you need is in your hands, and the power is within you. All that remains is the choice: will you believe? The answer to that question will define your journey from here. Success starts with the courage to believe—and I believe in you.

References

Introduction

- Brown, Brené. 2010. *The Gifts of Imperfection: Let Go of Who You Think You're Supposed to Be and Embrace Who You Are.* Hazelden Publishing.
    - A foundational book on resilience, authenticity, and self-acceptance, providing insights into how intentional practices can lead to personal transformation.
- David, Susan. 2016. *Emotional Agility: Get Unstuck, Embrace Change, and Thrive in Work and Life.* Avery.
    - Explores the importance of self-awareness, acceptance, and resilience, offering practical guidance on navigating life's challenges with agility.
- Dispenza, Joe. 2017. *Becoming Supernatural: How Common People Are Doing the Uncommon.* Hay House.
    - Covers the science of neuroplasticity, resilience, and personal transformation, demonstrating the potential of intentional practices to shape well-being.
- Fredrickson, Barbara L. 2001. The Role of Positive Emotions in Positive Psychology: The Broaden-and-Build Theory of Positive Emotions. *American Psychologist* 56(3): 218–226.
    - Discusses how positive emotions can enhance resilience, build lasting resources, and support overall well-being.

- Kabat-Zinn, Jon. 2013. *Full Catastrophe Living: Using the Wisdom of Your Body and Mind to Face Stress, Pain, and Illness.* Bantam.
    - A foundational work on mindfulness-based stress reduction, providing tools for cultivating mindfulness, resilience, and self-awareness in challenging situations.
- Linehan, Marsha M. 2015. *DBT Skills Training Manual* (2nd ed.). Guilford Press.
    - This manual includes exercises for building emotional regulation and resilience, essential for approaching well-being as a skill.
- Neff, Kristin. 2011. *Self-Compassion: The Proven Power of Being Kind to Yourself.* William Morrow.
    - A guide on practicing self-compassion and resilience, offering evidence-based strategies for maintaining emotional well-being through life's difficulties.
- Seligman, Martin E. P. 2011. *Flourish: A Visionary New Understanding of Happiness and Well-Being.* Atria Books.
    - This work on positive psychology explores the components of flourishing, emphasizing that well-being is achievable through intentional practices.
- Siegel, Daniel J. 2010. *Mindsight: The New Science of Personal Transformation.* Bantam.
    - Explores how mindfulness and self-awareness can transform the brain and foster emotional resilience, supporting well-being as a learnable skill.
- Tugade, Michele M. and Barbara L. Fredrickson. 2004. Resilient Individuals Use Positive Emotions to Bounce Back from Negative Emotional Experiences. *Journal of Personality and Social Psychology* 86(2): 320–333.
    - Examines how positive emotions contribute to resilience, supporting the idea that well-being can be cultivated through intentional emotional practices.
- VanderWeele, Tyler J. 2017. On the Promotion of Human Flourishing. *Proceedings of the National Academy of Sciences* 114(31): 8148–8156.

    - Discusses key factors that contribute to human flourishing, providing evidence for a comprehensive approach to building well-being.
- Williams, Mark and Danny Penman. 2011. *Mindfulness: An Eight-Week Plan for Finding Peace in a Frantic World.* Rodale Incorporated.
    - Covers mindfulness practices that foster resilience and self-awareness, essential for building well-being as a lifelong skill.

Chapter 1: What Is Well-Being?

- Davidson, Richard J. 2012. *The Emotional Life of Your Brain: How Its Unique Patterns Affect the Way You Think, Feel, and Live—and How You Can Change Them.* Hudson Street Press.
    - Neuroplasticity and the concept of well-being as a skill developed through practices like mindfulness, compassion, and gratitude.
- Seligman, Martin E. P. 2011. *Flourish: A Visionary New Understanding of Happiness and Wellbeing.* Atria Books.
    - Positive psychology framework on thriving, happiness, and well-being as more than the absence of distress.
- Kabat-Zinn, Jon. 2005. *Wherever You Go, There You Are: Mindfulness Meditation in Everyday Life.* Hachette Books.
    - Mindfulness meditation as a tool to build awareness and cultivate well-being.
- Lipton, Bruce H. 2008. *The Biology of Belief: Unleashing the Power of Consciousness, Matter & Miracles.* Hay House.
    - Epigenetics and the impact of choices on gene expression, aligning with the section on influencing genes through lifestyle and mindset.
- Davidson, Richard J. and Bruce S. McEwen. 2012. Social influences on neuroplasticity: Stress and interventions to promote well-being. *Nature Neuroscience* 15(5): 689–695.
    - The impact of practices such as mindfulness on brain circuits, supporting the idea that well-being can be cultivated.

- Dodge, Rachel, Annette P. Daly, Jan Huyton, and Lalage D. Sanders. 2012. The challenge of defining wellbeing. *International Journal of Wellbeing* 2(3): 222–235.
    - Provides a broad analysis of definitions for well-being, including distinctions between well-being, happiness, and wellness.
- HeartMath Institute. *The Science of Coherence*. Retrieved from https://www.heartmath.org/research/science-of-the-heart/
    - HeartMath's research on emotional coherence and resilience could support the sections on emotional resilience and building connection.

Chapter 2: Practice Makes Progress

- Brown, Brené. 2010. *The Gifts of Imperfection: Let Go of Who You Think You're Supposed to Be and Embrace Who You Are*. Hazelden Publishing.
    - Perfectionism, vulnerability, and the role of shame and fear, especially with the quote on perfectionism driving with shame and fear as passengers.
- Brown, Brené. 2012. *Daring Greatly: How the Courage to Be Vulnerable Transforms the Way We Live, Love, Parent, and Lead*. Gotham Books.
    - Vulnerability, courage, and the importance of showing up despite fear or failure.
- *Brené Brown via X on June 13, 2013.* https://x.com/BreneBrown/status/345178759856545792?lang=en
- Duckworth, Angela. 2016. *Grit: The Power of Passion and Perseverance*. Scribner.
    - Grit and the importance of persistence, resilience, and showing up to make progress, aligning with the themes of resilience and consistent effort.

- Seligman, Martin E. P. 2011. *Flourish: A Visionary New Understanding of Happiness and Wellbeing*. Atria Books.
    - Positive psychology concepts of growth, thriving, and resilience, relating to practicing resilience as part of well-being.
- Collins, Jim. 2001. *Good to Great: Why Some Companies Make the Leap… and Others Don't*. Harper Business.
    - Concepts related to 'failing forward' and the innovative, adaptive culture of organizations, mirroring the narrative of a start-up thriving through resilience and innovative practices.
- Maxwell, John C. 2007. *Failing Forward: Turning Mistakes into Stepping Stones for Success*. HarperCollins Leadership.
    - The concept of 'failing forward', using failure as a learning opportunity, and adapting to improve outcomes.
- Schwartz, Barry. 2004. *The Paradox of Choice: Why More Is Less*. Harper Perennial.
    - Managing expectations and dealing with perfectionism, aligning with the discussion of perfectionism versus excellence.
- Neff, Kristin. 2011. *Self-Compassion: The Proven Power of Being Kind to Yourself*. William Morrow.
    - Aligns with the idea of accepting imperfections and not striving to meet everyone's expectations, including one's own.
- Dweck, Carol S. 2006. *Mindset: The New Psychology of Success*. Random House.
    - Growth mindset and viewing failures as opportunities for growth, reinforcing the concept of resilience and failing forward.
- Duckworth, Angela L. and Quinn, Patrick D. 2009. Development and validation of the Short Grit Scale (Grit-S). *Journal of Personality Assessment* 91(2): 166–174.

- Measurement of grit and persistence, reinforcing the idea of perseverance in skill development and resilience.
- Seligman, Martin E. P. and Mihaly Csikszentmihalyi. 2000. Positive psychology: An introduction. *American Psychologist* 55(1): 5–14.
  - Foundational concepts of positive psychology, which include resilience and the pursuit of personal excellence over perfectionism.

Chapter 3: Practice Self-Awareness

- Dispenza, Joe. 'Doctor Joe Dispenza: Your Thoughts Are Making You Sick! You MUST Do This Before 10am To Fix It!' on *The Diary Of A CEO* with Steven Bartlett, August 14, 2023. https://podcasts.musixmatch.com/podcast/the-diary-of-a-ceo-with-steven-bartlett-01gtgefvr0avgejrkdemyqkfya/episode/doctor-joe-dispenza-your-thoughts-are-making-you-sick-01h7sdtx7rbnzah4pyvs70f99t
  - Quotation emphasizing the transformative power of self-awareness and the empowerment that comes with self-knowledge.
- Brown, Brené. 2012. *Daring Greatly: How the Courage to Be Vulnerable Transforms the Way We Live, Love, Parent, and Lead.* Penguin Random House.
  - Explores the role of vulnerability in self-awareness and building authentic connections.
- Goleman, Daniel. 1995. *Emotional Intelligence: Why It Can Matter More Than IQ.* Bantam Books.
  - Highlights the importance of emotional self-awareness and regulation as foundational for personal growth and relational impact.
- Tasha, Eurich. 2017. *Insight: Why We're Not as Self-Aware as We Think, and How Seeing Ourselves Clearly Helps Us Succeed at Work and in Life.* Crown Currency.

- Discusses the dual nature of self-awareness (internal and external) and offers strategies for gaining clearer insight into oneself.

- Dweck, Carol S. 2006. *Mindset: The New Psychology of Success.* Random House.
  - Introduces the growth mindset concept, essential for developing a flexible and adaptive approach to strengths and weaknesses.
- Collins, Jim. 2001. *Good to Great: Why Some Companies Make the Leap . . . and Others Don't.* HarperBusiness.
  - Covers the value of self-awareness in leadership, focusing on understanding one's strengths and weaknesses to drive growth and impact.
- Seligman, Martin E. P. 2002. *Authentic Happiness: Using the New Positive Psychology to Realize Your Potential for Lasting Fulfillment.* Free Press.
  - Explores strengths-based development and its role in fostering authentic personal growth and happiness.
- Neff, Kristin. 2011. *Self-Compassion: The Proven Power of Being Kind to Yourself.* William Morrow.
  - Discusses how self-compassion supports self-awareness by encouraging honest self-reflection without harsh self-criticism.
- Penman, Danny and Mark Williams. 2011. *Mindfulness: An Eight-Week Plan for Finding Peace in a Frantic World.* Rodale Books.
  - Covers mindfulness practices that foster resilience and self-awareness, essential for building well-being as a lifelong skill.

Chapter 4: Practice Positive Self-Narratives

- Brown, Brené. 2010. *The Gifts of Imperfection: Let Go of Who You Think You're Supposed to Be and Embrace Who You Are.* Hazelden Publishing.

    - Positive self-narratives, vulnerability, and self-compassion, aligning with the discussion on reframing narratives.
- Tolle, Eckhart. 2004. *The Power of Now: A Guide to Spiritual Enlightenment*. New World Library.
    - The concept of reframing narratives by focusing on present awareness and moving beyond past limitations.
- Dweck, Carol S. 2006. *Mindset: The New Psychology of Success*. Random House.
    - Growth mindset, which relates to adopting a positive self-narrative and shifting from a scarcity to an abundance mindset.
- Emerson, Ralph W. 1983. *Self-Reliance and Other Essays*. Dover Publications.
    - Concepts of self-determination and empowerment, similar to the idea that we are the authors of our self-narratives.
- Covey, Stephen R. 1989. *The 7 Habits of Highly Effective People: Powerful Lessons in Personal Change*. Simon & Schuster.
    - Discussion on abundance versus scarcity mentality, which ties into the reframing of self-narratives.
- Carver, Charles S. and Michael F. Scheier. 1982. Control theory: A useful conceptual framework for personality-social, clinical, and health psychology. *Psychological Bulletin* 92(1): 111–135.
    - Self-narratives in personal control and optimism, supporting the shift from a scarcity mindset to an abundance mindset.
- Seligman, Martin E. P. 1998. Learned optimism. *Journal of Personal and Social Psychology* 65: 50-64.
    - Learned optimism as a tool for reframing negative narratives and fostering a positive outlook.

Chapter 5: Practice Positive Rituals

- Clear, James. 2018. *Atomic Habits: An Easy & Proven Way to Build Good Habits & Break Bad Ones*. Avery.

- Core concepts of habit formation, micro habits, and the compounding effect of small, consistent actions.

- Duhigg, Charles. 2012. *The Power of Habit: Why We Do What We Do in Life and Business*. Random House.
  - The importance of habits in shaping outcomes and creating rituals for achieving goals.
- Nagoski, Emily and Amelia Nagoski. 2019. *Burnout: The Secret to Unlocking the Stress Cycle*. Ballantine Books.
  - The stress cycle and the role of movement in completing it, addressing the physiological nature of stress.
- Emmons, Roberts A. 2007. *Thanks! How Practicing Gratitude Can Make You Happier*. Houghton Mifflin.
  - The impact of gratitude on well-being, reinforcing the practice of gratitude as a daily ritual.
- Csikszentmihalyi, Mihaly. 1990. *Flow: The Psychology of Optimal Experience*. Harper & Row.
  - Concepts around creating fulfilling routines and experiences, aligning with the power of positive rituals for personal growth.
- Seligman, Martin E. P. 2002. *Authentic Happiness: Using the New Positive Psychology to Realize Your Potential for Lasting Fulfillment*. Free Press.
  - Positive rituals and practices like gratitude and generosity, supporting sustainable happiness and resilience.
- Sapolsky, Robert M. 2004. *Why Zebras Don't Get Ulcers: The Acclaimed Guide to Stress, Stress-Related Diseases, and Coping*. Holt Paperbacks.
  - Insights into the physiological effects of stress and the importance of movement in stress relief.
- Seligman, Martin E. P., Tracy A. Steen, Nansook Park, and Christopher Peterson. 2005. Positive psychology progress: Empirical validation of interventions. *American Psychologist* 60(5): 410–421.
  - Positive psychology interventions, including gratitude and other practices that enhance happiness and well-being.

- Lyubomirsky, Sonja, Kennon M. Sheldon, and David Schkade. 2005. Pursuing happiness: The architecture of sustainable change. *Review of General Psychology* 9(2): 111–131.
  - The sustainability of happiness through habits and routines, supporting the role of daily positive rituals in shaping life satisfaction.
- Harvard Health Publishing. 2024. *Understanding the stress response*. Retrieved from https://www.health.harvard.edu/staying-healthy/understanding-the-stress-response.
  - Explanation of the stress response, linking to the importance of movement in managing stress.
- Mayo Clinic Staff. (n.d.). *Gratitude: How being thankful can make you happier*. Retrieved from https://www.mayoclinic.org
  - The benefits of gratitude on mental health, emphasizing the role of gratitude as a daily positive ritual.

Chapter 6: Practice Mindfulness and Meditation

- Goleman, Daniel and Richard J. Davidson. 2017. *Altered Traits: Science Reveals How Meditation Changes Your Mind, Brain, and Body*. Avery.
  - The effects of meditation on the brain, neuroplasticity, and the long-term benefits of mindfulness practices.
- Dispenza, Joe. 2014. *You Are the Placebo: Making Your Mind Matter*. Hay House.
  - The science of brain-heart coherence and the connection between focused attention and intention in meditation practices.
- Kabat-Zinn, Jon. 1990. *Full Catastrophe Living: Using the Wisdom of Your Body and Mind to Face Stress, Pain, and Illness*. Delta.
  - Foundational practices in mindfulness and meditation, including mindfulness-based stress reduction (MBSR).
- Fredrickson, Barbara L. 2009. *Positivity: Top-Notch Research Reveals the 3-to-1 Ratio That Will Change Your Life*. Crown Archetype.

    - The broaden-and-build Theory and the positive effects of meditation on resilience and stress management.
- Nagoski, Emily and Amelia Nagoski. 2019. *Burnout: The Secret to Unlocking the Stress Cycle*. Ballantine Books.
    - Insights into completing the stress cycle and the physiological effects of stress management techniques, including movement and meditation.
- Doidge, Norman. 2007. *The Brain That Changes Itself: Stories of Personal Triumph from the Frontiers of Brain Science*. Viking.
    - The brain's ability to rewire itself through practices like meditation, highlighting the concept of 'neurons that fire together, wire together'.
- Goleman, Daniel. 1995. *Emotional Intelligence: Why It Can Matter More Than IQ*. Bantam Books.
    - The role of emotional intelligence in mindfulness and the effects of mindfulness on emotional regulation and empathy.
- Davidson, Richard J. and Bruce S. McEwen. 2012. Social influences on neuroplasticity: Stress and interventions to promote well-being. *Nature Neuroscience* 15(5): 689–695.
    - The impact of mindfulness and meditation on neuroplasticity and resilience.
- Keltner, Dacher and Jonathan Haidt. 2003. Approaching awe, a moral, spiritual, and aesthetic emotion. *Cognition and Emotion* 17(2): 297–314.
    - The role of awe in reducing inflammation and promoting mental and emotional health.
- Tang, Yi-Yuan., Britta K. Hölzel, and Michael I. Posner. 2015. The neuroscience of mindfulness meditation. *Nature Reviews Neuroscience* 16(4): 213–225.
    - Key brain regions affected by meditation, including the prefrontal cortex, amygdala, and hippocampus.
- HeartMath Institute. (n.d.). *The Science Behind Heart Coherence*. Retrieved from https://www.heartmath.org
    - Research on heart-brain coherence and the physiological benefits of positive emotions and heart-focused meditation.

- Mayo Clinic Staff. (n.d.). *Meditation: A Simple, Fast Way to Reduce Stress.* Retrieved from https://www.mayoclinic.org
    - Health benefits of meditation and mindfulness, including stress reduction and improved emotional well-being.

Chapter 7: Practice Drawing Healthy Boundaries

- Brown, Brené. 2018. *Dare to Lead: Brave Work. Tough Conversations. Whole Hearts.* Random House.
    - A comprehensive guide on leading with integrity and the role boundaries play in fostering trust and courage in relationships and leadership.
- Cloud, Henry and John Townsend. 1992. *Boundaries: When to Say Yes, How to Say No to Take Control of Your Life.* Zondervan.
    - A foundational work that explores the concept of boundaries, how to establish them, and the impact they have on healthy relationships.
- Dispenza, Joe. 2017. *Becoming Supernatural: How Common People Are Doing the Uncommon.* Hay House.
    - Covers the science behind personal energy, values, and decision-making, offering insights into aligning personal actions with core beliefs.
- Fredrickson, Barbara L. 2001. The Role of Positive Emotions in Positive Psychology: The Broaden-and-Build Theory of Positive Emotions. *American Psychologist* 56(3): 218–226.
    - Examines how positive emotions, such as those fostered by healthy boundaries, enhance personal resilience and help build lasting resources for well-being.
- Goleman, Daniel. 1995. *Emotional Intelligence: Why It Can Matter More Than IQ.* Bantam Books.
    - Discusses self-awareness, empathy, and emotional intelligence, including the role of boundaries in personal and professional settings.

- Linehan, Marsha M. 2015. *DBT Skills Training Manual* (2nd ed.). Guilford Press.
  - This manual on Dialectical Behaviour Therapy (DBT) includes tools for setting boundaries, managing interpersonal conflicts, and practicing self-care.
- Nagoski, Emily and Amelia Nagoski. 2019. *Burnout: The Secret to Unlocking the Stress Cycle.* Ballantine Books.
  - Focuses on completing the stress cycle, with practical advice on using boundaries to prevent burnout and protect emotional well-being.
- Neff, Kristin and Christopher Germer. 2018. *The Mindful Self-Compassion Workbook: A Proven Way to Accept Yourself, Build Inner Strength, and Thrive.* Guilford Press.
  - Provides exercises for practicing self-compassion, understanding personal needs, and setting compassionate boundaries to support personal growth.
- Schwartz, Shalom H. 1992. Universals in the Content and Structure of Values: Theoretical Advances and Empirical Tests in 20 Countries. *Advances in Experimental Social Psychology* 25: 1-65.
  - An academic study examining the universality and personal significance of values, which serve as a basis for setting personal boundaries.
- Tartakovsky, Margarita. 2016. Why Setting Boundaries Is Important (and 4 Ways to Start). *Psych Central.*
  - A practical article outlining why boundaries are essential for well-being and offering simple strategies for setting them.
- Hasson, G. 2021. *The Self-Care Handbook: Practical Ways to Prioritize You.* Octopus Publishing Group.
  - Explores the necessity of self-care through boundaries, offering exercises and reflections for setting limits that support mental and emotional health.

- Williams, Mark and Danny Penman. 2011. *Mindfulness: An Eight-Week Plan for Finding Peace in a Frantic World.* Rodale Books.
    - Discusses mindfulness techniques that support boundary-setting, helping readers build self-awareness and recognize personal needs without guilt.

Chapter 8: The Power of Believing

- Ford, Henry. 1947. *Today and Tomorrow*. Doubleday, Page & Company.
    - Explores Henry Ford's philosophy of innovation, leadership, and the importance of belief in achieving success.
- Dweck, Carol S. 2007. *Mindset: The New Psychology of Success.* Ballantine Books.
    - A groundbreaking book on the impact of fixed versus growth mindsets, emphasizing how belief in personal growth fosters achievement.
- Doidge, Norman. 2007. *The Brain That Changes Itself: Stories of Personal Triumph from the Frontiers of Brain Science.* Viking.
    - A deep dive into neuroplasticity and how repeated thought patterns can reshape the brain, supporting the power of belief to drive change.
- Shinn, Florence S. 1925. *The Game of Life and How to Play It.* Martino Fine Books.
    - Highlights the role of affirmations and belief in shaping one's reality and achieving success.
- Brown, Brené. 2012. *Daring Greatly: How the Courage to Be Vulnerable Transforms the Way We Live, Love, Parent, and Lead.* Avery.
    - Discusses the role of vulnerability, self-awareness, and belief in building authentic and fulfilling lives.
- Kabat-Zinn, Jon. 1990. *Full Catastrophe Living: Using the Wisdom of Your Body and Mind to Face Stress, Pain, and Illness.* Delacorte Press.

- Explains the role of mindfulness and meditation in rewiring beliefs to promote emotional resilience and well-being.

- Goleman, Daniel. 1995. *Emotional Intelligence: Why It Can Matter More Than IQ*. Bantam Books.
  - Highlights the connection between emotional awareness, belief systems, and the ability to navigate challenges effectively.
- Clear, James. 2018. *Atomic Habits: An Easy & Proven Way to Build Good Habits & Break Bad Ones*. Avery.
  - A practical guide on creating small, consistent actions to reinforce empowering beliefs and drive personal transformation.
- Peale, Norman V. 1952. *The Power of Positive Thinking*. Prentice Hall.
  - An influential work on how belief, faith, and positive thought can shape outcomes and improve quality of life.
- Frankl, Victor E. 2006. *Man's Search for Meaning*. Beacon Press.
  - A profound exploration of the role belief and purpose play in finding fulfillment and resilience, even in the most challenging circumstances.
- Tolle, Eckhart. 2005. *A New Earth: Awakening to Your Life's Purpose*. Penguin Group.
  - Explores the power of belief in transcending the ego and aligning with a deeper sense of purpose.
- Seligman, Martin E. P. 2011. *Flourish: A Visionary New Understanding of Happiness and Well-being*. Free Press.
  - A foundational text on the science of positive psychology, focusing on how belief in one's ability to thrive contributes to lasting well-being.
- Loehr, Jim and Tony Schwartz. 2003. *The Power of Full Engagement: Managing Energy, Not Time, Is the Key to High Performance and Personal Renewal*. Free Press.
  - Discusses how belief and intentional focus transform energy into sustained productivity and fulfilment.

- Covey, Stephen R. 1989. *The 7 Habits of Highly Effective People: Powerful Lessons in Personal Change*. Free Press.
    - Emphasizes how belief in core principles and values drives effective habits and long-term success.
- Hill, Napoleon. 1937. *Think and Grow Rich*. The Ralston Society.
    - A classic work highlighting how belief, desire, and persistence fuel success in personal and professional endeavours.
- Dispenza, Joe. 2019. *Breaking the Habit of Being Yourself: How to Lose Your Mind and Create a New One*. Hay House.
    - A scientific and practical guide to rewiring beliefs through thought, emotion, and action to create a new reality.
- Cuddy, Amy. 2015. *Presence: Bringing Your Boldest Self to Your Biggest Challenges*. Little, Brown Spark.
    - Examines the role of belief in shaping confidence and presence, supported by body language and mindset.
- Emmons, Robert A. 2007. *Thanks!: How the New Science of Gratitude Can Make You Happier*. Houghton Mifflin.
    - Explores the connection between gratitude, belief in abundance, and improved well-being.
- Lipton, Bruce H. 2005. *The Biology of Belief: Unleashing the Power of Consciousness, Matter & Miracles*. Hay House.
    - Explores the science behind how beliefs influence biology, highlighting the mind-body connection in personal transformation.
- Siegel, Daniel J. 2010. *Mindsight: The New Science of Personal Transformation*. Bantam Books.
    - A deep exploration of how mindfulness and belief can reshape neural pathways, fostering healing and growth.